GU

J. Matthew Sleeth, MD

SERVING GOD

A Call to Care for Creation and Your Soul

SAVING THE PLANET

Twelve Sessions

ZONDERVAN®

ZONDERVAN.com/
AUTHORTRACKER
follow your favorite authors

We want to hear from you. Please send your comments about this book to us in care of zreview@zondervan.com. Thank you.

ZONDERVAN

Serving God, Saving the Planet Guidebook
Copyright © 2010, 2012 by Blessed Earth and Dot&Cross

This title is also available as a Zondervan ebook. Visit www.zondervan.com/ebooks.

Requests for information should be addressed to:

Zondervan, *Grand Rapids, Michigan* 49530

ISBN 978-0-310-68870-9

All Scripture quotations, unless otherwise indicated, are from the *New Revised Standard Version of the Bible,* copyright © 1989 by the Division of Christian Education of the National Council of Churches of Christ in the United States of America, and are used by permission. All rights reserved.

Scripture quotations marked NIV are taken from The Holy Bible, *New International Version®, NIV®.* Copyright © 1973, 1978, 1984, 2011 by Biblica, Inc™. Used by permission. All rights reserved worldwide.

Scripture quotations marked NLT are taken from the *Holy Bible, New Living Translation,* copyright © 1996, 2004. Used by permission of Tyndale House Publishers, Inc., Wheaton, Illinois. All rights reserved.

Any Internet addresses (websites, blogs, etc.) and telephone numbers in this book are offered as a resource. They are not intended in any way to be or imply an endorsement by Zondervan, nor does Zondervan vouch for the content of these sites and numbers for the life of this book.

Written by Matthew Sleeth, Nancy Sleeth, and Michael Colletto
Edited by Michael Colletto
Cover design: Ron Huizinga
Cover photography: Noel Hendrickson/Getty Images®
Interior design: David Conn

Printed in the United States of America

12 13 14 15 16 17/DCI/ 20 19 18 17 16 15 14 13 12 11 10 9 8 7 6 5 4 3 2

CONTENTS

HOW TO USE THIS STUDY

The *Serving God, Saving the Planet* film series is designed to challenge God's people to think critically and biblically about the issue of creation care. Whether you are exploring this issue on your own or within a group at home, school, or church, don't feel like you have to read every section or answer every question in this guidebook. Take your time, set your own pace, and simply open your heart to God. Allow Him to use this material to change your life.

FOR INDIVIDUALS

If you have access to your own copy of the DVD and wish to explore the content in greater depth on your own, we recommend that you watch each film session first, then work through the corresponding session of this guidebook. If you have time, watch the film a second time to continue to flesh out your answers.

FOR GROUPS

If you're sharing a copy of the DVD and exploring the sessions in a group setting, we recommend that you read through each session first in preparation for your group discussion.

Before the session: Read the session in advance. This guidebook was designed to be easy to understand, so you'll be able to answer many of the questions without having seen the films. Answer as many questions as you can (but don't feel like you have to answer them all). Fill out the Action Plan for today and this year. If you'd rather, simply make a few notes as you read through — whatever helps you feel prepared to meet with your group.

During the session:

1. Watch the film together.
2. If the group is large (more than 10 people), divide into discussion groups of six or fewer. Discuss the session and share your answers and action plans. Do not feel like you must get to every question.
3. If you split up the group, bring everyone back together to share highlights from your discussions and share one or more goals with the whole group.
4. Assign the next session.

FOR GROUP LEADERS

You do not need to be a teacher or "expert" to lead a group — you just need a desire to share the call to care for creation and your souls. If you're interested in leading a group discussion, please visit blessedearth.org and download the free Leader's Guide for additional ideas and instructions.

Thank you for sharing this journey with us. We are grateful for all you are doing to care for God's creation!

— Matthew and Nancy Sleeth

INTRODUCTION

Most of us are familiar with the story of creation recorded in Genesis. In six days, God created all the elements of the world — light, water, land and vegetation, the heavens, animals, and, finally, man. When everything was complete, God stood back and sized up what He'd created … and He declared that it was good — very good.

Because God believes in the value of the world, we should too. Everything God created is worthy of being cared for and protected. In the first six sessions of *Serving God, Saving the Planet*, we will explore how we can show our love for God and for our neighbors by caring for His creation. My personal journey began when I started examining the Bible in the context of God's creation, and it's changed me forever.

In the final six sessions of *Serving God, Saving the Planet*, we will explore how we live out Christ's love. We'll be focusing not on nouns, but on verbs — on actions. As members of the "body" of Christ we act as the hands and feet of God's will on the planet. If God loves the world, we should too.

This isn't about you saving the planet. It's not about you trying really hard to do things right so God won't punish you. It's about your heart. If your heart is overflowing with the love of God, if your heart beats with His, your life — like Christ's — will be different. And your care, compassion, and joyful generosity will breathe hope into a world groaning for redemption.

Ultimately, *Serving God, Saving the Planet* is about a radical, biblical truth: following Jesus is good for the whole earth — the planet itself and its entire people. In the end, hope for today and hope for tomorrow is found in nothing less than our God at work in us. In His grace and power, may we learn to be better stewards of all He's entrusted into our care.

— Dr. Matthew Sleeth, Executive Director, Blessed Earth

Session 1

LIGHT

SESSION SUMMARY

> *"In the beginning, God created the heavens and the earth. Now the earth was formless and empty, darkness was over the surface of the deep, and the Spirit of God was hovering over the waters. And God said, 'Let there be light,' and there was light."*
>
> **—Genesis 1:1-3 NIV**

This was the beginning of the beginning—the moment when God chose to create a universe for His own glory. God speaks the first sentence of a love story that will include all creatures and all people throughout all the ages ... and it all begins with light.

Everyone we know and everything we see starts with God speaking light into existence. Scripture is full of references to light: light is used to represent God's goodness (Psalm 56:13), a guide (Psalm 43:3), and the truth (John 3). God Himself is light (1 John 1:5). So, it's not surprising that when God sends His only begotten Son, He is called the "Light of the World" who conquers all darkness. And we, as followers of Jesus, are called to be children of light (Ephesians 5) and the light of the world (Matthew 5).

In choosing to follow Christ, we become new people with new priorities. God changes our hearts ... and our behaviors change, too. It's not about following a list of rules; it's about fol-lowing the lifestyle of Jesus.

Just before Jesus left this earth, He said, "Go into the world and preach the gospel to all the creatures, baptizing them in the name of the Father, the Son, and the Holy Spirit and teaching them to obey everything I've commanded you." The very first commandment we were given in the Bible is recorded in Gen-esis 2:15. We were told to tend and care for this garden — the earth. We can't go out and make disciples while simultaneously destroying the water, the air, and the creatures that God loves. If we don't respect the world around us, we're missing a major part of what God commanded us to do.

It's time for the church, as children of the light, to take a lead-ership role in caring for the planet. And it will be good.

REFLECTIONS ON LIGHT

My first scientific encounter with light occurred in kindergarten. I can't recall my teacher's name, but I remember the experiment we conducted.

Our class filled two clay pots with dirt. We planted bean seeds in both pots and watered them. We then placed one pot in a closet and shut the door and put the other outside in a court-yard, in the sunshine.

After a number of days, both plants sent up shoots — and for a short while they resembled each other. Both grew on the energy stored within the planted seed. As the days passed, the plant in the sun began to change. It turned green and beautiful. The plant in the dark closet continued to grow for awhile, but it looked pale and spindly. It never produced any fruit or seeds of its own.

What I learned in kindergarten is that life runs on sunshine. Irrespective of whether it's you, me, or a tree, life on earth is dependent on the element of light.

When we give ourselves over to God, we step from darkness into a great light. The light is necessary for beauty, growth, and bearing fruit. We cannot supply the light on our own any more than the plant in the closet can make itself green.

— Dr. Matthew Sleeth

SESSION NOTES: LIGHT

As you watch the first film session on *Light*, feel free to use the space below to jot down any notes, thoughts, and questions.

SESSION QUESTIONS: LIGHT

1

Why do you think the creation story begins with light?

"And God said, 'Let there be light,' and there was light. God saw that the light was good, and he separated the light from the darkness."

— Genesis 1:3-4 NIV

2

Can you recall an experience when light made you feel closer to God—through an inspiring sunrise, rainbow, light sheeting through the clouds, or sunset? Describe the scene and what it taught you about God.

"When we behold the light and brightness of the sun, the golden edges of an evening cloud, or the beauteous rainbow, we behold the adumbrations of His glory and goodness, and in the blue sky, of His mildness and gentleness."

— Jonathan Edwards (1703-1758),
Reflections of Glory

3

Dr. Sleeth explains, "As the light of the world, Jesus is a beacon for all of us. He's a model of how to live, how to conduct our everyday life." In what sense is Jesus a model for our everyday choices?

4

What does it mean to become a "child of the light"? What actions are "light" and what actions are "dark" in terms of caring for creation?

"Jesus asks us to become children of light."

— Dr. Matthew Sleeth

5

A regular incandescent bulb wastes 90 percent of the energy it consumes producing heat instead of visible light. In what ways do we waste our energy and not produce the light that God wants us to?

6

By contrast, an energy-efficient bulb uses about 90 percent of the energy going in to make light. It's light that we can do something by. In practical terms, how does stewarding our resources more wisely show our love for God and our neighbors around the world?

A CHANGED HEART = A CHANGED LIFE

Caring for God's creation intersects with every aspect of our Christian walk, including how we steward electricity and light. If we can do 10 percent better each year, we are headed in the right direction!

Matthew has always been obsessed with light; our home has been the testing ground for lighting technology. We have tried every new kind of light bulb on the market, going back more than twenty years to those first energy-saving bulbs that buzzed and gave off a harsh light. When we moved the last time, a friend jokingly suggested that we start a Museum of Light Bulb History.

▶ **Energy-saving light bulbs use about one-quarter the energy of standard light bulbs and last up to ten times longer.**

If you have been reluctant to buy energy-saving light bulbs because you think they give off an unflattering light, give the new "soft" and "warm" bulbs a try. Their light is indistinguishable from regular light bulbs. Plus, the wide selection of bulbs available today makes it possible to find the right energy-saving bulb for every imaginable wattage and fixture. Several light bulb manufacturers even make CFLs designed for use in candelabras and on dimmer switches.

Energy-saving bulbs do cost more initially, but the average payback in energy savings takes less than a year—even sooner if you use rebates or find bulbs on sale. Conventional bulbs are the most energy-intensive, followed by halogens, then compact fluorescents. The most efficient bulbs are light-emitting diode (LED) bulbs.

Turning lights off when not in use is the easiest way to save energy. Dimming your lights also can cut back on electricity bills.

▶ **About 90 percent of the electrical current used to power standard light bulbs creates heat instead of light.**

This makes energy-saving bulbs not only vastly more efficient, but also much safer. According to an EPA Energy Star fact sheet, if every American home replaced just one standard light bulb with an energy-efficient bulb, we would save enough energy to light more than 3 million homes, retain more than $600 million in annual energy costs, and prevent offgassing equivalent to the emissions of more than 800,000 cars. Simply changing our light bulbs can also save lives that would otherwise be lost due to respiratory illnesses and asthma attacks caused by air pollution from coal-fired power plants, especially among children and senior citizens.

One common question about CFLs concerns the mercury they contain. It's true: a CFL bulb contains a minuscule amount of mercury (4 mg on average), about one-fifth of the mercury found in the average watch battery and less than 1/600th of the mercury found in a home thermostat. However, the amount they contain is small compared to the amount of mercury that coal-burning power plants emit to power the much-less-efficient incandescent bulb. A power plant will emit four times as much mercury to power a 60W incandescent bulb as compared to an equivalent CFL.

Those signs you see when you go fishing warning children and pregnant women to avoid eating the catch are not because of toxins dumped into the water. The concern over mercury poisoning comes primarily because of the mercury emitted from coal-fired power plants that settles in our rivers and lakes. To properly dispose of a burned-out CFL, just drop it off at a local Home Depot or IKEA store, or check out www.earth911.org for other safe disposal options.

The bottom line: using compact fluorescents cuts back on your electric bill, is safer for the environment, and better for people.

—Nancy Sleeth

Adapted with permission from *Go Green, Save Green: A Simple Guide to Saving Time, Money, and God's Green Earth* (Tyndale, 2009).

GOOD STEWARD ACTION PLAN: LIGHT

Instructions

1. Pick two or more new actions from the suggested lists to commit to today and this year — or come up with your own ways to conserve light and electricity.
2. Go to blessedearth.org and join our community of Good Stewards. Explore the website to find additional ideas for saving energy and becoming a better steward of God's creation.
3. We will send encouragements to you and help you stay on track with your goals. We're all in this together, so share your journey. Let us know what was easy, and what was difficult; inspire others with your story!

TODAY, LORD, HELP ME TO:

Pick at least two of the following goals, or come up with your own actions.

○ Turn off lights when I leave the room.
○ Rely on natural light as much as possible.
○ Memorize at least one Scripture about light (use a Bible concordance if needed).
○ Pray for the millions of people in the world who live without a reliable source of electricity.
○ Pray for the millions of people in the world who exist in spiritual darkness.

1. _____

2. _____

THIS YEAR, LORD, HELP ME TO:

Pick at least two of the following goals, or come up with your own actions.

○ At night, walk through my house with a flashlight and note how many lights are left on 24/7 (computers, audio equipment, etc.). Eliminate as many as possible by plugging these appliances into power strips and turning them completely off when not in use.

○ Switch at least seven incandescent bulbs to energy-efficient bulbs. (LED are best, then CFL, then halogen, then dimmable or lower wattage incandescent.)

○ Encourage family and coworkers to turn off lights when they leave the room.

○ Place at least one Scripture about light in a place that I see often (on the refrigerator, on my computer, next to an outlet or light switch).

1. _____

2. _____

"I love the symbolism of beginning our Genesis 2:15 journey by changing light bulbs."

—Dr. Matthew Sleeth

Session 2

WATER

SESSION SUMMARY

> *"And God said, 'Let there be a vault between the waters to separate water from water.' So God made the vault and separated the water under the vault from the water above it. And it was so."*
> **—Genesis 1:6–7 NIV**

Water is an indispensable building block of life. Our very bodies consist mostly of water. Without water, life on this planet would not exist.

God was extravagant with water—He covered nearly two-thirds of the planet with it. Some people have described the earth as a "water planet."

But there's a problem: 97 percent of the water on earth is saltwater—the briny, ocean water we all remember tasting as a child on our first trip to the beach. And there's a second problem—about 85 percent of our fresh water is locked up in polar icecaps. This means that of all the water on earth, less than one half of 1 percent is drinkable and accessible to us. Fresh water is relatively rare!

Yet water is so much more than a physical necessity of life. It's a symbol that Christ uses over and over again to describe

Himself. Water is God's symbol of rebirth, His metaphor for resurrection to a new life.

Jesus Himself was baptized in the water of the Jordan River as a symbol of what was to come, a physical death and a resurrection to eternal life.

Being a good steward means we must recognize the powerful role water plays in our lives, physically and spiritually.

REFLECTIONS ON WATER

I was meeting with a group of graduate students from around the world. In a relaxed moment, the students started talking about what they found most striking about American culture. They brought up the size of our grocery stores, our religious and ethnic tolerance, and our friendliness.

One woman explained that she was from a small farming village on the Korean peninsula. When she came to school in the U.S., it was her first time out of her rural setting. What is it like to live in rural Asia for decades and then suddenly be beamed up to urban America? "What strikes me as the most amazing thing," she said, "is that in America everyone empties their bladder in gallons of pure drinking water."

Her cheeks blushed, and she looked around the room to see what the reaction would be.

One flush of the average American toilet is more fresh drinking water than one third of the world uses in a day. As access to clean water becomes increasingly rare, followers of Christ must become better stewards of this precious gift.

— Dr. Matthew Sleeth

SESSION NOTES: WATER

As you watch the second film session on *Water*, feel free to use the space below to jot down any notes, thoughts, and questions.

SESSION QUESTIONS: WATER

1

Although nearly two-thirds of the planet is covered in water, very little is drinkable and accessible. Why is fresh water precious? In what ways do we take it for granted?

"Say you fill a bathtub with about thirty gallons of water. Of that thirty gallons, one gallon would represent the fresh water on earth. And of that one gallon, one teaspoon would represent the amount that's drinkable and accessible. In other words, out of an entire bathtub, one teaspoon represents all the fresh water on earth that we can get to."

— Dr. Matthew Sleeth

2

Dr. Sleeth comments that "in addition to serving its utilitarian purpose, water can be a source of great joy." Recall a particularly significant time in your life involving water and describe how it made you feel.

3

Dr. Sleeth lists some examples of water being used in the Old Testament: "Moses hits a rock and water comes out. Jonah is propelled to Nineveh. God parts the Jordan for Joshua's army to go through and uses water to select Gideon's 300 warriors. The prophet Elisha uses water to cure Naaman's leprosy. Rebekah watering the camels at the well is a sure sign of her beautiful and kind heart."

Reflect on the significance of one of these (or another) Old Testament reference to water.

4

Water plays an equally important role in the New Testament. Jesus' first recorded miracle is to turn water into wine. He calms the sea when it's stormy and his disciples are in the boat. Jesus even walks on water to show His control over nature.

Reflect on the significance of one of these (or another) New Testament reference to water.

5

When Jesus meets the Samaritan woman at the well, He tells her, "Everyone who drinks from this well will be thirsty again, but whoever drinks the water that I have, they will never thirst again." How can the "living waters" that Jesus offers help quench our thirst for material things?

6

Why do most of us say a prayer of thanks when we eat a meal, but not when we brush our teeth, turn on the shower, or wash our clothes? How can saying a prayer of thanks alter our stewardship habits?

"I try to appreciate water now. It's a gift rather than just an entitlement. For much of my life, I thought water was just something that came out of the hose or the sink. But it's so much more than that. All over the world, there are millions of people who have to walk miles just to get a single jug of water. They dig wells, they plant, and they simply have to pray for the rains to come."

— Dr. Matthew Sleeth

A CHANGED HEART = A CHANGED LIFE

Last summer, we visited a friend on his family land in eastern Tennessee. After our picnic, I dipped a five-gallon bucket into the barrel that connects to a rainspout on the roof and started to carry water to their newly planted saplings. After the first round, I realized that five gallons was too heavy for me to carry any significant distance, so I started filling the bucket halfway full. Despite the drought, they had enough water collected in the makeshift rain barrel to bring several gallons to each young tree.

Driving home, I told Matthew that I had never really thought about how much water weighs and how much energy it must take to pump it up from the river and to our home. It takes about 3.5 gallons to flush a traditional (pre-1992) toilet, and about 1.6 gallons to flush a low-flow toilet. Imagine if we had to carry that water from several miles away, like the people Matthew met when practicing medicine in Honduras. I think I would be much more careful about the water I pour down the drain.

The Bible is full of references to women drawing water from wells — women like Rebekah, who was kind to God's creatures and remembered to water the camels, and the Samaritan woman with five husbands, who met Jesus and found eternal life. These women were reminded daily that water is a gift from God, not something to take for granted when we turn on the tap.

Carrying those pails of water to the saplings reminded me that it's not just water we conserve when we take shorter showers; it's also the energy it takes to transport that water. It requires loving and grateful hearts to appreciate the gifts right before us.

▶ **The average U.S. household consumes about twice as much water every day as the average home in Britain.**

There are a lot of simple changes you can make to save water inside the home. For example, something as simple as turning off the faucet while brushing teeth and shaving can save a family of four about 48 gallons of water a day. Also:

Install low-flow showerheads. If you tried a low-flow shower-head years ago and were not satisfied—try again. They've improved dramatically. Readily available at hardware and home improvement stores, low-flow showerheads can cost less than $10, and installation can be done by a homeowner.

Only run the dishwasher and clothes washer with full loads. We have an energy-efficient front-load washer, which not only saves electricity and water, but also spins out most of the moisture, so clothes dry much more quickly. Use the coldest water setting that gets the job done, and don't wash items such as pants, skirts, dresses, and sweaters every time you wear them—they'll last longer and you'll save time, water, and energy.

Fix leaky and inefficient toilets. Toilets are the biggest water users in the home. A leaky toilet can waste 200 gallons of water every day. Also, if you do not have an efficient toilet, try inserting a couple of bricks or 1-liter bottles filled with water in the toilet tank to reduce the amount of water wasted with each flush.

▶ **As much as 40 percent of our drinking water is flushed down toilets.**

To reduce water waste outside in our lawns and gardens, one of the simplest things you can do is reclaim your water. By collecting water that has been used for bathing or other household duties and using it to water your plants, you can save up to 300 gallons per month. Or go one step further and install a rain barrel to collect water from your downspouts.

Also, use a spray nozzle on your garden hose to save up to 6.5 gallons per minute and, instead of using regular sprinklers, water your flowerbed and garden using drip irrigation or a soaker hose. This method saves water by minimizing evaporation and watering only the base of your plants. Similarly, mulching your plants reduces the amount of water lost through evaporation, limits weed growth, and improves soil conditions.

—Nancy Sleeth

Adapted with permission from *Go Green, Save Green: A Simple Guide to Saving Time, Money, and God's Green Earth* (Tyndale, 2009).

GOOD STEWARD ACTION PLAN: WATER
Instructions

1. Pick two or more new actions from the suggested lists to commit to today and this year — or come up with your own way to be a better steward of water.
2. Go to blessedearth.org and join our community of Good Stewards. Explore the website to find additional ideas for saving water and becoming a better steward of God's creation.
3. We will send encouragements to you and help you stay on track with your goals. We're all in this together, so share your journey. Let us know what was easy, and what was difficult; inspire others with your story!

TODAY, LORD, HELP ME TO:
Pick at least two of the following goals, or come up with your own actions.

O Turn off the faucet while shaving and brushing teeth.
O Cut shower time by at least three minutes.
O Only run the dishwasher and clothes washer when full.
O Memorize at least one Scripture about water (use a Bible concordance if needed).
O Pray for the millions of people in the world who live without a reliable source of water.

1. _____

2. _____

THIS YEAR, LORD, HELP ME TO:

Pick at least two of the following goals, or come up with your own actions.

O Install low-flow showerheads and sink aerators.

O Fix leaky faucets and toilets.

O Check to see if I have an older toilet that uses three gallons or more per flush; if so, place several liter bottles filled with water in the tank to displace some of the water.

O Use dishwater to water plants.

O Place at least one Scripture about water in a place that I see often (on my bathroom mirror, next to the kitchen faucet, near the dishwasher or clothes washer).

O Compost instead of using the garbage disposal.

O Think before I buy anything, and buy used when possible. Most items use huge quantities of water in the manufacturing process.

O Find out about organizations (such as Charity Water) that help people in poor countries who don't have access to clean water and pray about how I can help.

1. _____

2. _____

"We are deeply worried to see that entire peoples, millions of human beings, have been reduced to destitution and are suffering from hunger and disease because they lack drinking water. In fact, hunger and many diseases are closely linked to drought and water pollution. In places where rain is rare or the sources of water dry up, life becomes more fragile; it fades away to the point of disappearing."

—Pope John Paul II, Speech in Brazil,
Lenten Message, 1993

Session 3

SOIL

SESSION SUMMARY

> *"I am the vine; you are the branches. If you re-*
> *main in me and I in you, you will bear much fruit;*
> *apart from me you can do nothing."*
> — John 15:5 NIV

One of the few parables that Jesus overtly explains is the story
of the four soils. As we sow seeds, some fall on the path and are
eaten by birds; these are the truths that we hear and the devil
takes away. The seeds that fall on the rock are truths that sprout,
but wither in hard times because they have no root to sustain them.
The seeds that grow up with the thorns are eventually choked out;
these represent the cares and the emails and the current events
that distract us from God. But the seeds that fall onto good soil
yield good fruit in abundance—this is the soil that pleases God.

God wants us to grow in our faith, like trees planted in good
soil. Trees are mentioned hundreds of times in the Bible. Wherever there's a tree, a branch, a bush, a vine, or a stick on the
page, it's a safe bet that God is at work. At the center of the
Garden of Eden are two of the most important trees: the Tree of
Life and the Tree of Knowledge. God speaks to Moses through
a burning bush. Moses holds up a branch to part the Red Sea.
Abraham meets the angels under the oaks of Mamre. Deborah

holds court under a palm tree. Nathanael prays beneath the trees when Jesus calls him to be a disciple.

All of these scriptural references to trees, branches, and vines call us to bear fruit in our lives. Jesus describes the fruit of the Spirit as love, joy, peace, patience, kindness, goodness, faithfulness, gentleness, and self-control. When our actions are filled with the fruit of the Spirit, we are in a right relationship with God, our neighbors, and His creation. Jesus is the vine, and we are the branches. Apart from Him, we cannot become better stewards of creation; but with Him, all things are possible.

REFLECTIONS ON SOIL

In my women's spiritual group, we decided to each write down a question for everyone to answer as a way of getting to know each other better. One member of the group wrote: "Describe a miracle in your life."

What a great invitation! I listened as the young woman seated to my right described her miracle. She had been raised in an affluent community where everyone in her neighborhood had gardens, but no one she knew grew food. Just out of college and equipped with a degree in finance, something (or Someone) led her to purchase a five-inch tomato plant. Moving the plant to her patio, she wondered how that weak little stem could ever support a full-grown tomato. Every day after work, she sat on the patio and stared at the plant. She continued to watch in amazement as the plant grew and developed flowers. Soon, little green balls appeared, grew ever larger, and then slowly blushed crimson.

Watching that tomato plant grow changed her heart. In awe of God's creation and no longer desiring the career she had prepared for in banking, she started learning about a totally different form of currency. In a series of conversations, her pastor discussed ways she could live out her faith not just on Sundays, but in her everyday life. These two revolutionary ideas—that people could work to grow their own food and grow their own faith—merged.

She learned as much as she could about sustainable agriculture, quit her job, and interned with an organic farmer. Over the last five years, she's worked for environmental nonprofits and started community gardens.

God used one tomato plant to change a life—now that's what I call miraculous.

—Nancy Sleeth

Adapted with permission from Go Green, Save Green: A Simple Guide to Saving Time, Money, and God's Green Earth (Tyndale, 2009).

SESSION NOTES: SOIL

As you watch the third film session on *Soil*, feel free to use the space below to jot down notes, thoughts, and questions.

SESSION QUESTIONS: SOIL

1

God has a special relationship with all of creation, but especially with trees. Trees are mentioned hundreds of times in the Bible. Reflect on one or more events in the Bible that involve trees, branches, or vines (examples: the Tree of Life, the burning bush, the cross). What do they teach us?

2

What do you believe Nikephoros of Chios (1750-1821) meant when he said that people would "become poor because they will not have a love for trees.... If you don't love trees, you don't love God"?

3

Planting a tree is an investment in the future; the trees you enjoy today are gifts from prior generations. Describe a tree that has given you joy. Are you planting trees for future generations?

"Even if you are old, you must plant. Just as you found trees planted by others, you must plant them for your children."

—4th century writing

4

Dr. Sleeth said, "When I chose to follow Jesus, He made it clear that I needed to make some changes in my life. And if you choose to [become a follower of Jesus], you've got to make changes, too."

What changes in your life have you made since becoming a follower of Jesus?

5

One leader warned Dr. Sleeth that he should never mention the word "sacrifice" when speaking about caring for creation. Sacrifice, however, is the cornerstone of our faith. How can sacrifice become a key component of solving some of our environmental problems?

"The seriousness of ecological degradation lays bare the depth of man's moral crisis.... Simplicity, moderation and discipline, as well as the spirit of sacrifice, must become a part of everyday life."

— Pope John Paul II (1920 – 2005), *Peace with God, Peace with Creation*

6

If you simplified your life, what would be the hardest thing for you to give up?

"People will often ask, 'What was the hardest thing to give up?' They expect me to say 'my car' or 'my house' or 'my paycheck.' But, for me, it was my social status."

—Dr. Matthew Sleeth

7

How are "things" keeping you from a Christ-focused life?

"The most beautiful part was that one by one, my wife and my children all became followers of Christ. We were on the same page, serving the same God with the same priorities. We found that the fewer possessions we owned, the less things owned us."

—Dr. Matthew Sleeth

A CHANGED HEART = A CHANGED LIFE

I didn't always love gardening. I grew up in the suburbs and, every spring, my dad had a load of steaming mulch dumped in our driveway. It was the children's job to shovel the mulch into the wheelbarrow and spread it evenly around the trees and bushes. When we finally scraped up the last shovelful, our yard looked beautiful ... but gardening had sunk to the bottom of my list of desired vocations.

By the time I was twelve or thirteen, I'd discovered a way to avoid most outdoor work: my mom would rather weed in the sunshine than be tied to the kitchen, so I traded outside chores for fixing dinner.

I was twenty years old when Matthew and I married — by then I was skillful in the kitchen, but still had no desire to be a gardener. For the first seven years of our marriage, we mostly lived in apartments where gardening was not an option.

My attitude adjustment occurred during Matthew's residency. Our next-door neighbors had been raised in a Mennonite farming community. Thinking it would be fun to grow some of our own food with our young children, we decided to start a garden together.

The house where we lived already had a small garden plot adjacent to the garage. I planted easy-to-grow carrots, tomatoes, radishes, and peas — not enough to feed a family, but the look on our son Clark's face when he pulled up his first carrot was payment enough for my effort. Later we added corn and squash in my neighbor's plot. Growing food fit my frugal nature, and it got me out of the house. I was hooked.

After Matthew finished his residency, we moved to northern New England. Although the growing season there is short, people plant magnificent perennial gardens. Thanks to neighbors who offered to give me divisions from their plants, I was able to plant a spring-to-fall succession of blooms. Next to my vegetable garden, I planted blueberry bushes and a small orchard.

The biggest shift in my gardening practices, however, came when we built our house in New Hampshire.

▶ **There are 30 million acres of "mowable" lawns in the U.S., and 66 million U.S. households own at *least* one lawnmower. Altogether, U.S. lawnmowers use 580 million gallons of gasoline each year.**

So, instead of planting grass, I sowed two thirds of an acre with wildflower seed. The field thrived and attracted wildlife — birds, deer, wild turkeys … and tourists. Strangers stopped to ask if they could photograph and paint the field. Neighbors were invited to pick bouquets. Churches used our wildflowers for special occasions.

▶ **Homeowners spend a total of $29 billion annually on professional lawn care.**

Two friends helped us construct raised beds for my vegetable garden. The vegetable garden was so successful the first summer that we decided to double it in size the next, and double it again the next. By the third year, we were growing enough potatoes, carrots, onions, and tomatoes to last year-round. Clark and Emma often weeded with me in the early morning. Matthew used our pressure cooker to can our bounty. It was a family enterprise.

When we moved to Kentucky, one of my first priorities was preparing a small organic garden on the south side of our house. We've used the garden for teaching college students basic gardening skills, from preparing the earth all the way to harvest. Yet sometimes I still feel very much like an amateur gardener, with so much yet to learn.

Matthew's family grew and raised the majority of their food for economic reasons, so for a long while, gardening brought back not-so-fond memories for him of picking potato bugs off plants. But recently, Matthew has joined me in the garden. Come evening, when we work in comfortable silence among the rows, it feels like Paradise restored: just as God intended, husband and wife together, tending and caring for the Lord's earthly garden.

—Nancy Sleeth

Adapted with permission from *Go Green, Save Green: A Simple Guide to Saving Time, Money, and God's Green Earth* (Tyndale, 2009).

GOOD STEWARD ACTION PLAN: SOIL
Instructions

1. Pick two or more new actions from the suggested lists to commit to today and this year — or come up with your own way to care for the earth.
2. Go to blessedearth.org and join our community of Good Stewards. Explore the website to find additional ideas for becoming a better steward of God's creation.
3. We will send you encouragements throughout the year and help you stay on track with your goals. We're all in this together, so share your journey. Let us know what was easy, and what was difficult; inspire others with your story!

TODAY, LORD, HELP ME TO:
Pick at least two of the following goals, or come up with your own actions.

O Spend at least five minutes seeing only what God has created. If necessary, I will close off my field of vision to a six-inch patch of nature, and meditate on His goodness. "Be still, and know that I am God."

O Research organizations (Floresta, Restoring Eden Project, Heifer Project) that plant trees in developing countries and ask God how I can help.

O Find out about local parks and outdoor activities that my family might enjoy.

O Check the weather forecast and schedule a good night for viewing stars.

O Take a walk outdoors.

1. _____

2. _____

THIS YEAR, LORD, HELP ME TO:

Pick at least two of the following goals, or come up with your own actions.

O Purchase local, organic food.

O Hang a bird feeder in a tree near my window.

O Do something out of the ordinary outdoors, such as get up early to take a sunrise walk, feed the ducks in my local park, or go on a picnic.

O Bring a bag when I go for a walk and pick up any trash I see.

O Rake leaves instead of collecting them with a blower or mower.

O Start a compost pile.

O Mow the lawn lower and less frequently.

O Look into faith-based environmental organizations — such as Blessed Earth, A Rocha, and the Evangelical Environmental Network — and pray about how I can get involved.

1. _____

2. _____

"When my dad talks to groups about the need to care for creation, he's often asked, 'Isn't this environment thing kind of low on the list of Christian priorities? What if Jesus comes back today?' Dad usually answers by telling a story about the reformer Martin Luther. Apparently, Luther once gave a Sunday morning sermon about the second coming of Christ. He was such a powerful preacher that when his parishioners went home, they all started acting as if Jesus were going to return that afternoon. One man from the church happened to walk by Luther's house and saw him planting a tree. The parishioner was puzzled and asked him if he really believed his own sermon, shouldn't he be doing what he'd want to be doing when Jesus returns? Luther answered that planting a tree was exactly what he wanted to be caught doing when the Lord came back. I'd have to say 'Amen.' If Jesus came back this afternoon, I'd rather be tending to God's beautiful creation than doing just about anything else."

— Emma Sleeth, daughter of Matthew and Nancy

Adapted with permission from *It's Easy Being Green: One Student's Guide to Serving God and Saving the Planet* (Zondervan/Youth Specialties, 2008).

Session 4

HEAVENS

SESSION SUMMARY

"He counts the stars and calls them all by name.
How great is our Lord! His power is absolute! His
understanding is beyond comprehension"
—Psalm 147:4-5 NLT

God created a universe of wonder for us to enjoy. He gave us the sun and the moon for warmth and light and stars to help us find our way. On the one hand, these heavenly bodies are reassuring, giving order to our days, our seasons, and our yearly calendar. On the other hand, they are full of mystery beyond our comprehension.

Both of these aspects of the night sky teach us about the face of God. The heavens show us that God cares about every detail of our lives; God knows the name of every star, just as He knows every hair on our head. At the same time, the vastness of the heavens reminds us just how small we are, keeping us humble before our Creator. The universe is filled not only by stars and solar systems, but by untold billions of galaxies.

When we look up at the night sky, we get a glimpse of just how big God is. He's a God who can speak galaxies into existence; He can create extravagant, over-the-top beauty in the farthest reaches of space ... and provide the moon to help us find our way home on a dark night. He's with us when we feel lost and small and scared and alone.

It's not by accident that a star announces the birth of the infant Christ. And on the last page of the Bible, Christ describes Himself as the "bright morning star." If you ever begin to think that maybe God's love isn't quite big enough to save a people or a planet as messed up as we are, stare into the night sky and—just like Abraham—try to count the stars.

God calls us to trust that He is present in all the mysteries of life. When we embrace the mystery of the heavens, we begin to understand a little bit more about the nature of God.

REFLECTIONS ON HEAVENS

It's my parents' fault that Matthew and I moved to New England.

For two weeks every August, my family went camping. One summer when I was about eleven or twelve, we camped at Sebago Lake in Maine. What I remember most from that trip were the shooting stars. Every night, we went down to the docks and stared up at the heavens. No Hollywood movie or concert could compete with the free show we watched on those cool, starry nights.

When Matthew and I were first married, I took him to New England to see "real stars." We stayed at a lakeside cottage that belonged to friends of my parents. The stars were even better than I remembered. Matthew was hooked.

After Matthew's residency, we spent a dozen years living in Maine. Many summer nights, we brought blankets out onto the back deck and watched the comets streak across the sky. Often the kids fell asleep there, tucked into sleeping bags. What could be more pleasant and secure than Daddy carrying you in his arms up to bed, all the while dreaming of God's diamonds in the sky?

—Nancy Sleeth

Adapted with permission from *Go Green, Save Green: A Simple Guide to Saving Time, Money, and God's Green Earth* (Tyndale, 2009).

SESSION NOTES: HEAVENS

As you watch the fourth film session on the *Heavens*, feel free to use the space below to jot down notes, thoughts, and questions.

SESSION QUESTIONS: HEAVENS

1

Dr. Sleeth describes some of his favorite memories looking up at the night sky—as a child, husband, and parent. What memories do you associate with the night sky?

2

The heavens also give order to our lives. Describe some of the ways that the heavens provide a rhythm to the days, seasons, and yearly calendar of your life.

"When I consider your heavens, the work of your fingers, the moon and the stars, which you have set in place, what is mankind that you are mindful of them, human beings that you care for them?"

—Psalm 8:3–4 NIV

3

The book of Job contains the longest soliloquy by God in the Bible. God asks Job, "Can you direct the movement of the stars—binding the cluster of the Pleiades or loosening the cords of Orion? Can you direct the sequence of the seasons or guide the Bear with her cubs across the heavens? Do you know the laws of the universe? Can you use them to regulate the earth?" What does this passage teach us about humility?

"The heavens declare the glory of God; the skies proclaim the work of his hands."
—Psalm 19:1 NIV

4

The church father Athanasius (297-373) wrote in *On the Incarnation of the Word of God*, "Nothing in creation has erred from the path of God's purpose for it, save only man. Sun, moon, stars, water, air, none of these has swerved from their order, but, knowing the Word as their Maker and their King, remained as they were made. Men alone, having rejected what is good, have invented nothings instead of the truth."

In relation to our current stewardship of God's creation, in what ways have we "swerved" and "rejected what is good"?

5

In addition to inspiring awe, the heavens can offer hope. In context of creation care, how can we, in the words of the apostle Paul, "shine like stars in the universe" amidst "a crooked and depraved generation"?

"So that you may become blameless and pure, children of God without fault in a warped and crooked generation. Then you will shine among them like stars in the sky as you hold firmly to the word of life."

—Philippians 2:15–16 NIV

A CHANGED HEART = A CHANGED LIFE

A friend of Emma's recently told me that he rarely looks to see if the stars are visible at night. "I just don't think about it," he said. "My dad said he and his friends could find all the constellations and would play late into the night under the stars, but I didn't grow up that way."

This young man is not alone. When I spoke at a college in Texas, I asked how many of the students in the audience had seen the Milky Way. Only a few hands went up. I have found this to be true in colleges all over the country:

▶ **Three fourths of Americans grow up never having seen the Milky Way.**

In the last two centuries, we've obscured the Milky Way that Abraham, Isaac, Jacob, Jesus, and Paul all knew so well by filling the night sky with manmade light.

While artificial light certainly has benefits, it also has consequences—something called light pollution. Light pollution is caused in large part by poor lighting design—artificial light shining upward and outward toward the sky rather than focusing downward, where it is needed.

From space, all of Europe and Japan and most of America can be seen as a glowing dome of light.

▶ **In satellite photos taken at night, we can see that at least two thirds of humanity lives under light-polluted skies.**

Here on earth, even on the clearest nights, most city residents can no longer view the stars. Instead, they have grown accustomed to a ubiquitous orange haze, while the glorious heavens created by God continue to shine, undisturbed and unheeded.

When we disrupt God's natural rhythm of light and dark, the migration, reproduction, and feeding of life on earth is affected. Along the coasts, sea turtles have a harder time finding darkened beaches for nesting. Frogs and toads living near highways artificially made as much as a million times brighter than normal have their nighttime breeding songs thrown out of kilter. Whole flocks of winged creatures exhaust themselves trying to escape the maze of city lights.

Artificial light also harms humans. Our regular pattern of waking and sleeping—called circadian rhythms—are fundamental to mental and physical well-being. As an emergency room physician, I often worked twenty-four-hour shifts. ER docs are not alone—today nearly one fifth of the world population works in shifts. The resulting lack of regular sleep and rest is not conducive to a healthy home life, or a healthy body. Hypertension, peptic ulcer disease, cardiovascular mortality, higher incidences of work-related accidents and car accidents, depression, drug and alcohol abuse, and higher divorce rates are more common in shift workers. Life expectancy for shift workers is reduced by as much as four years. Is our twenty-four-hour productivity quota really worth the toll?

By short-circuiting our sensitivity to God's patterns of light and dark, we are blindly experimenting with human health as well as the health of every living creature on earth. But here's the good news:

▶ **Of all the forms of pollution facing the world today, light pollution is probably the most easily fixed.**

Simple changes in lighting design and installation translates to immediate reductions in the amount of light we pour out into the atmosphere. As a bonus, these changes also save us energy. Hundreds of communities throughout the U.S. now use covered street fixtures that light only the ground below rather than wastefully shining it in all directions. At home, porch lights that are tucked into ceilings and outdoor motion detectors can ensure safety while reducing waste.

Light pollution (and air pollution in general) interferes with stargazing. But something else often gets in the way: we are often so worn out from our busy schedules that we don't take time to connect with the natural world. Slow down. Shut off the TV, close the laptop, and linger outdoors in the evenings for a change. Switch off the porch lights, spread a blanket on the lawn, and try to count the stars, just as Abraham did. As you gaze upward, you cannot help but be filled with humility and the wonder of God's creation.

—Dr. Matthew Sleeth

GOOD STEWARD ACTION PLAN: HEAVENS
Instructions

1. Pick two or more new actions from the suggested lists to commit to today and this year — or come up with your own ways to curb light pollution and conserve electricity.
2. Go to blessedearth.org and join our community of Good Stewards. Explore the website to find additional ideas for becoming a better steward of God's creation.
3. We will send you encouragements throughout the year and help you stay on track with your goals. We're all in this together, so share your journey. Let us know what was easy, and what was difficult; inspire others with your story!

TODAY, LORD, HELP ME TO:
Pick at least two of the following goals, or come up with your own actions.

○ Turn off lights in rooms that are not in use.
○ Direct light to where it is needed instead of flooding general areas; use a lamp instead of an overhead light for reading or enjoying a meal; use less light wherever possible.
○ Turn off all lights before going to bed.
○ Spend a few minutes outside tonight, looking at the stars; ask God to reveal how I can become a better steward of His creation.

1. _____

2. _____

THIS YEAR, LORD, HELP ME TO:

Pick at least two of the following goals, or come up with your own actions.

- ○ Reserve activities that require a lot of lighting, such as painting walls, artwork, sewing, and cleaning to the daytime hours when the sun provides a light source instead of trying to do work under intense lights at night.
- ○ Install motion detectors for outdoor lighting.
- ○ Consider installing motion detector lights inside, especially in rooms where the lights are left on often.
- ○ Use dimmer LED nightlights instead of regular incandescent bulbs.
- ○ At night, keep the light inside and don't let the glow out; shut the blinds, draw the drapes, and dim the switches when possible.

1. _____

2. _____

"Dear heavenly Father, please help me become a better steward of Your creation, on earth as it is in heaven. As I stare in awe at the night sky, fill my heart with humility and wonder. I praise You for the daily miracle of light and darkness, work and rest. Thank You most of all for the gift of Your Son, the Bright Morning Star, in whose name I pray."

—Nancy Sleeth

Session 5

ANIMALS

SESSION SUMMARY

> *"But ask the animals, and they will teach you,*
> *or the birds in the sky, and they will tell you; or*
> *speak to the earth, and it will teach you, or let*
> *the fish in the sea inform you. Which of all these*
> *does not know that the hand of the LORD has*
> *done this? In his hand is the life of every crea-*
> *ture and the breath of all mankind."*
>
> **—Job 12:7-10 NIV**

God is in the life business. It's his desire that the sky and the air teem with creatures. He allowed Adam the privilege and responsibility of naming each creature, and He entrusts us with their stewardship. We are charged with caring for and protecting the habitats they depend upon for survival.

Even though God has entrusted us with stewardship of animals, the reality is that He still holds the deed to the planet. It's therefore not surprising that compassion for animals is associated with godly people, such as Noah, Moses, Rebekah, and Laban. In contrast, people such as Levi and Simeon are cursed not only because they are cruel to humans, but because they are cruel to animals.

Jesus, our model for compassion, is called the Good Shepherd and "the firstborn of all creatures." He's born in a manger surrounded by animals, and His first visitors are shepherds who have come to see the Lamb of the World. After Jesus is baptized, the Holy Spirit descends upon Him like a dove. Christ gets His taxes out of the mouth of a fish and He rides into Jerusalem on the back of a colt. There's an intimate connection between Jesus and God's creatures.

As followers of Christ, we should love what God loves. When we care about every bird in the sky as deeply as our Father, He is pleased.

REFLECTIONS ON ANIMALS

It's been a dreadfully hot summer, so I haven't gone on my favorite hike down to the river very often in the last couple of months. But today, the temperature (if not the humidity) dropped a bit, so I decided to make the journey. My glasses fogged up repeatedly, and some much-needed rain dampened my body and clothes, but my soul, as always, was lifted by this time in God's creation.

On this hike the easy part comes first; I hike down for the view. The view is not some grand vista—just a gently moving river. Always—always!—I find the river to be quietly comforting.

Deep in prayer today, I was startled on my way back up the hill, not by the flock of birds or silent deer that I sometimes disturb, but by the buzz of a bumblebee darting around my head. In between my footsteps, muffled by leafy carpets, I heard the starlings singing. They seemed to be saying, "This is God's woods; not yours, not mine."

I have read arguments by some academicians that animals know, but man knows that he knows. In other words, it's our ability to reflect on what we know that makes us more intellectually sophisticated than the squirrels I heard chattering above me in the woods.

And yet, though we are "smarter," animals have much to teach us. Watching those squirrels jump from branch to branch reminds me that every step I take is no less a leap of faith. The squirrels' seemingly impossible acrobatics are only made possible by the very same hand that holds me up every moment of every day. We, like these forest creatures, must place our ultimate trust in God, just as our offspring trust in us.

The walk in the woods teaches me what animals—and children—instinctively know: that God is fully present all around us, if only we pause long enough to see.

—Nancy Sleeth

Adapted with permission from Go Green, Save Green: A Simple Guide to Saving Time, Money, and God's Green Earth (Tyndale, 2009).

SESSION NOTES: ANIMALS

As you watch the fifth film session on *Animals*, feel free to use the space below to jot down notes, thoughts, and questions.

SESSION QUESTIONS: ANIMALS

1 What does the animal kingdom teach us about the Creator?

"Nothing is without order and purpose in the animal kingdom; each animal bears the wisdom of the Creator and testifies of Him."

— John Climacus (509 - 603)

2 Dr. Sleeth says that we are "given dominion of animals, which implies a tremendous amount of responsibility." Have you ever been given dominion over an animal, such as a pet? What did you learn from that responsibility?

3

Throughout Scripture, God expresses His desire for us to care for animals. On the Sabbath day, God commanded the Israelites to give their animals rest (Exodus 2:10). In the year of rest for the land, they were to allow livestock and wild animals to eat from their fallow fields (Exodus 23:11; Leviticus 25:7). How do our actions harm the habitats that animals need in order to survive?

"The righteous care for the needs of their animals, but the kindest acts of the wicked are cruel."

—Proverbs 12:10 NIV

4

God commanded the Israelites to help when an ox or donkey had fallen over, or was carrying a burden too heavy for it to bear (Exodus 23:5; Deuteronomy 22:4). In addition, livestock were also allowed to eat as they worked (Deuteronomy 25:4). Finally, God says to us in Proverbs 27:23: "Be sure you know the condition of your flocks, give careful attention to your herds." Most of us are not shepherds or farmers today, but we can still show respect for animals. How can our purchasing power help animals be treated fairly?

5

God promises a long life to those who will watch over wild birds (Deuteronomy 22:6-7). In Job 38:41, God says that He hears the newborn ravens crying to Him for food. Jesus explains that God supplies food for the wild birds and that not one sparrow falls to the ground without Him noticing (Matthew 6:26; 10:29). What can these scriptural references to birds teach us and what can we learn from observing birds?

"We can learn much about God by placing a bird feeder in our yard."
— John Stott

6

Have you ever seen someone being cruel to an animal? As stewards of creation, why does this upset us?

"Compassion, in which all ethics must take root, can only attain its full breadth and depth if it embraces all living creatures and does not limit itself to humankind."
— Albert Schweitzer (1875-1965)

A CHANGED HEART = A CHANGED LIFE

Open spaces are important for the survival of all of God's creatures. As stewards of God's creation, it is important for us to preserve the habitats that animals need to survive.

We live in an interrelated, interconnected world. To get our 99-cent burgers at the fast-food drive-through, for example, we cut down South American rainforests so our cattle can graze. As a consequence, with no tree roots to hold down the topsoil, the land becomes barren in just a few years and poverty increases. The air grows more polluted because there are no trees to cleanse the air. Without clouds forming over South America or rain falling on Africa, droughts worsen, leading to widespread hunger and starvation. These unintended consequences hurt poor people first and hardest; in addition, they devastate indigenous animal populations.

Underlying these problems is the belief that undeveloped land is of little value. As followers of Christ, all of creation has value. Moreover, Christians are instructed to love what God loves. God loves every sparrow and every lamb. If we value what God values, then we will learn to care for and preserve all of His creation.

No matter where you live, you can help create a nature preserve. Whether you are the steward of a 100-acre farm, a suburban backyard, a townhouse sliver of garden, or a high-rise balcony, animals need food, water, and shelter to thrive. Here are some ways you can help:

Food — Everyone needs to eat, even animals. One of the best investments we ever made is the two bird feeders we hung near our front window. The birds that visit have given us countless hours of enjoyment. You can also feed wildlife by including seeds from a plant, berries, nectar, foliage and twigs, nuts, fruits, sap, pollen, and suet in your garden plans.

Water — Wildlife need sources of clean water for many purposes, including drinking, bathing, and reproduction. Water sources include birdbaths, puddling areas for butterflies, and ponds or rain gardens. If you set up a birdbath, be sure to change the water two to three times per week during warm weather when mosquitoes are breeding, so that any eggs laid in the water don't have time to hatch.

Shelter — Wildlife needs places to hide from people, predators, and inclement weather. Shrubs, thickets, and brush piles provide great hiding places within their bushy leaves and thorns — and a safe place for wildlife to raise their young. Consider making a birdhouse for the types of birds you would like to attract to your habitat. Attracting pollinators, such as bats and bees, can also be beneficial to your garden.

Pesticides and Fertilizers — When we use chemicals on our lawns and gardens, we harm wildlife. If it's harmful to cats and dogs and wildlife, it can't be great for humans either. Many of the chemicals that we use on the lawn and garden end up being ingested by animals, and ultimately enter our food chain.

William McDonough, the dean of green architecture, measures the success of any project by the number of songbirds that remain when he is done. As followers of Christ, perhaps it's time for us to measure the beauty of our lawns and gardens by the birds and other wildlife they shelter, just as God shelters us.

— Nancy Sleeth

GOOD STEWARD ACTION PLAN: ANIMALS
Instructions

1. Pick two or more new actions from the suggested lists to commit to today and this year — or come up with your own way to care for animals.
2. Go to blessedearth.org and join our community of Good Stewards. Explore the website to find additional ideas for becoming a better steward of God's creation.
3. We will send encouragements to you and help you stay on track. We're all in this together, so share your journey. Let us know what was easy, and what was difficult; inspire others with your story!

TODAY, LORD, HELP ME TO:
Pick at least two of the following goals, or come up with your own actions.

○ Pray for the well-being of all of God's creatures, and for clarity about how I can live in harmony with them.

○ Go for a walk in a park or nature preserve.

○ Spend time quietly in nature observing animals.

○ Meditate on Mark 16:15: "He said to them, 'Go into all the world and preach the gospel to all creation'" (NIV).

○ Memorize a Scripture, such as Psalm 145:9, "The LORD is good to all; he has compassion on all he has made" (NIV).

1. _____

2. _____

THIS YEAR, LORD, HELP ME TO:

Pick at least two of the following goals, or come up with your own actions.

O Regularly eat at least one more meatless meal than usual.

O Avoid meat, eggs, and poultry raised by factory farms. Instead, seek out local, small farmers who raise animals compassionately.

O Learn about an endangered species and do something to help.

O Hang a bird feeder near a window. Black oil sunflower seed is a favorite of many seed-eating species.

O Look at the fertilizers that I normally use on my lawn and investigate if I can use less harmful substitutes.

O Go camping, hiking, and canoeing with children so they will appreciate all of God's creation.

O In winter, avoid cutting back dead flowers and foliage, which can serve as valuable food for wildlife. Leave dead stalks, leaves, and seedheads standing to feed wildlife and provide cover.

1. _____

2. _____

"My prayer is that we truly humble ourselves before God and His creation and strive to learn from His kingdom. May we have the wisdom to know the needs of the creatures that God created, and to care for them as God would care for them. May we learn to love them as God loves us."

— Dr. Matthew Sleeth

Session 6

HUMANITY

SESSION SUMMARY

*"The LORD God took the man and put him in the
Garden of Eden to work it and take care of it."*
—Genesis 2:15 NIV

In Genesis 2:15, God gave us our first job assignment: to tend and protect the Garden. One reason God wants us to take care of the planet is because we can't live without it. Our very survival depends upon the health of the planet.

Taking care of the planet is also a form of giving. Jesus said that the most important kind of giving isn't the kind that seeks recognition. It's about helping people who can't thank you. It's about sacrifice. It's about helping people who aren't even born yet. It's about planting seeds for the future.

Some people think we don't need to take care of the earth because it's all going to be destroyed. Why bother? Jesus could come back tomorrow. And they're right; Jesus could come back tomorrow. But if He doesn't come back for 10,000 years, think about how many people would get to hear the good news. Isn't that reason enough to take care of the world? Wasn't that reason enough for our great-great-grandparents to take care of the world? Someday Jesus will return, but until then, we're told to be the hands and feet of God here on earth.

If we believe in an all-powerful God, maybe we should ask ourselves this question: Why were we born here? Why weren't we just born in heaven? God placed us here because He wants us to choose Him. This life, this time, is a gift — it's a love story. God wants us to say, "I do," not, "I have to."

God designed each of us to be part of a vast body that stretches across time and space and culture. It's called the body of Christ — the church. God didn't leave His church, His body of Christ, floating out in the middle of nowhere. He left it on a planet teeming with life and teeming with hope. God's hope for creation rests in us.

REFLECTIONS ON HUMANITY

All of life on earth is precious — a gift from God. With this gift comes responsibility. Like any gift, it is to be cared for and appreciated.

As a physician, my job was to take care of people. In the emergency room, I saw a lot of what could go wrong with the human body.

It was not my job to judge the patient — only to treat the disease. If a finger was dangling off, I sewed it back on. If children came in with croup, I helped them breathe again. If a drunk got in a fight, I repaired the damage.

Diagnosing a problem and fixing it is good work; I found great satisfaction in sending people out of the ER in better shape than when they came in. But in some cases, I couldn't help thinking that it would have been even better if we could have prevented the damage in the first place.

The same is true for the earth. God is in the life-giving business. He has put all of creation in our care. We are to use the gifts He has given us, but never abuse them. We are to be good stewards of our own lives — and of all life on earth.

— Dr. Matthew Sleeth

SESSION NOTES: HUMANITY

As you watch the sixth film session on *Humanity*, feel free to use the space below to jot down notes, thoughts, and questions.

SESSION QUESTIONS: HUMANITY

1

How does taking care of the planet contribute to the health of our grandchildren?

"God wants us to take care of this planet, but I think there's something even more important to God than birds or trees or clean air. What's even more important to God is you and me and our children and our grandchildren and their grandchildren."

— Dr. Matthew Sleeth

2

Dr. Sleeth explains that "taking care of the planet is a form of giving." In what sense is this true? Who are we giving to?

3

In his *Commentary on Genesis*, John Calvin (1509-1564) wrote, "The custody of the garden was given to Adam, to show that we possess the things which God has committed to our hands, on the condition that, being content with the frugal and moderate use of them, we should take care of what shall remain."

Have recent generations been "content with the frugal and moderate use" of the earth's resources? Give examples.

4 How can Christians take a lead role in caring for the earth?

"It is not right for us to destroy the world God has given us. He has created everything; as the Bible says, 'The God who made the world and everything in it is the Lord of heaven' (Acts 17:24). To drive to extinction something He has created is wrong. He has a purpose for everything.... We Christians have a responsibility to take the lead in caring for the earth."

—Rev. Billy Graham, *Detroit Free Press*

5 How does repentance, humility, and seeking the face of God offer hope for the planet?

"If my people, who are called by my name humble themselves, pray, seek my face, and turn from their wicked ways; then I will hear from heaven, and will forgive their sin and will heal their land."

—2 Chronicles 7:14

A CHANGED HEART = A CHANGED LIFE

When we moved from New Hampshire to Kentucky, it gave us the opportunity to simplify by giving away a lot of stuff that was still cluttering our lives. Clothes went to The Salvation Army, art supplies to a kindergarten teacher, books to libraries hit by a hurricane, and tools to a church friend starting a second career as a carpenter.

Since moving in, we've made a number of cost-effective, simple changes to our new, old house. The first thing we did was change all the lightbulbs in the house to compact fluorescents. Matthew also put our stereo and our son's computer on a power switch, eliminating the phantom loads.

We needed to purchase a new washing machine and a refrigerator. At the local home center, I picked out a front-load washer. Using the Energy Star comparison tags, I also found a standard refrigerator that uses 445 kWh per year, much more efficient than others in its class. Matthew lowered the energy use of our new refrigerator even more by turning off the automatic icemaker.

We chose not to purchase a clothes dryer. Instead, Matthew restrung an abandoned clothesline in the backyard. Friends helped us dismantle an unsafe, rickety porch on the back of the house, and Matthew and our son, Clark, built a new one using decking made of recycled soda bottles, thus eliminating the need for toxic stains or paints.

I went to www.freecycle.org and found a free composting bin for the backyard, which eliminates the need to power a garbage disposal in the sink and makes an organic soil booster for the garden. I also used Freecycle to give away our moving boxes and some extra building materials. Thanks to Freecycle, someone else used whatever we didn't need — including the former deck stairs and extra lumber from the deck, which prevented scrap from going into the landfill.

Next, Matthew got busy on the glamorous part of conservation, changing a leaky float valve in the toilet and cutting the water used per flush in half by inserting several bricks and a milk jug filled with water into the toilet tanks. He also changed the showerhead to a low-flow model (purchased at the hardware store for about $5), turned the water heater to its lowest setting, and then put insulation on the accessible basement piping. The insulation looks like black foam tubing and slips around the pipes quite easily. These toilet and shower projects only took a couple of hours and will save both energy and water for years to come.

The old single-pane aluminum windows in the house were a huge area of thermal gain and loss. We could not afford to replace them right away, but I greatly improved their efficiency by making heavy, lined drapes for all the windows. The attic only had three inches of insulation, so we increased it to R-60. (The higher the R-value, the more effective the insulation is in keeping a house warm in winter and cool in summer.) Matthew and Clark put soffit and ridge vents in to allow adequate airflow in the attic.

During a six-month period, our electric bill ranged from a high of $18 to a low of $13. The gas and water bills are similarly modest, thanks to these types of small changes throughout the house.

The kids and I planted apple, pear, peach, and cherry trees in our yard and started a vegetable garden on the south side of the house. The garden is prospering, thanks to a load of old manure from a neighbor's farm.

We fit a bicycle with a carrier made from an old milk crate, which makes it safe and convenient for us to run errands without using the car. But the most important energy-saving decision we made was the choice of our home's location. It is two blocks from our children's college, which has eliminated the need to fly them home for school breaks. We also chose a home that allows us to walk to the store, the bank, and work, which means far less time commuting and more time for family and ministry.

In our three decades together, one of the things Matthew and I have learned is that our home is about a whole lot more than Matthew and me. It is about our children, our calling, the example we set, and the legacy we leave.

— Nancy Sleeth

Adapted with permission from *Go Green, Save Green: A Simple Guide to Saving Time, Money, and God's Green Earth* (Tyndale, 2009).

GOOD STEWARD ACTION PLAN: HUMANITY
Instructions

1. Pick two or more new actions from the suggested lists to commit to today and this year — or come up with your own ways to fulfill the Genesis 2:15 call.
2. Go to blessedearth.org and join our community of Good Stewards. Explore the website to find additional ideas for saving energy and becoming a better steward of God's creation.
3. We will send encouragements to you and help you stay on track. We're all in this together, so share your journey. Let us know what was easy, and what was difficult; inspire others with your story!

TODAY, LORD, HELP ME TO:
Pick at least two of the following goals, or come up with your own actions.

O Avoid opening the refrigerator door before I know what I want; unplug refrigerators or freezers in the basement or garage that are not in use.

O Avoid using aluminum foil and plastic wrap.

O Turn my hot water heater to a lower setting.

O Learn about the recycling program in my area.

O Drink tap water instead of bottled water, sodas, or sports drinks.

O Read Psalms 23, 24, 104, 147, and 148.

O Ask God to help me become a better steward of His resources.

O Follow our grandmothers' advice: "Use it up, wear it out, make it do, or do without."

1. _____

2. _____

THIS YEAR, LORD, HELP ME TO:

Pick at least two of the following goals, or come up with your own actions.

O Cut up food into smaller pieces before cooking; put the lid on pans; match the size of the pan to the burner; cook outside in summer.

O Grocery shop only once a week. Combine trips. Carpool.

O Pre-cycle by not purchasing items with excessive packaging, individual wrapping, or packaging that can't be recycled.

O Reduce the amount of junk mail I receive by registering at www.dmaconsumers.org/cgi/offmailinglist.

O Switch to eco-friendly cleaning products, or find recipes for making my own at blessedearth.org.

O Use cloth towels instead of paper; switch to toilet paper and tissues made from recycled paper; avoid using paper plates and paper cups.

O Donate a box of books to the library.

O Find out if my electricity provider offers a green power option and make the switch.

O Wear pants, dresses, sweaters, and skirts several times before washing; iron clothes only when absolutely necessary.

1. _____

2. _____

Session 7

REST

SESSION SUMMARY

> *"All who keep the Sabbath without desecrating it
> and who hold fast to my covenant — these I will
> bring to my holy mountain and give them joy in
> my house of prayer."*
>
> **— Isaiah 56:6 - 7 NIV**

On the seventh day God created rest. He didn't just stop creating things; He created something new, blessed it, and called it holy. And so we begin our series of actions with the indispensable inaction of a day of rest.

Rest doesn't just happen. It's not just the absence of activity. Rest, like all good things, is a gift from God in and of itself. The fourth commandment is really quite simple: stop everything. Relax. *"Remember the Sabbath and keep it holy."* It's the only commandment that begins with "Remember," as if God knew we would forget about it. It's also the longest of the Ten Commandments. God is explicit and all-inclusive: don't work on the Sabbath day — don't make your son or daughter or anyone else in your household work, don't make strangers or illegal aliens or minimum-wage employees work, and don't make animals work. Everyone and everything gets a day of rest. We cool our jets. We idle our engines.

Sounds nice, but how do we find rest in a 24/7 world? Just as the Hebrew people were slaves in Egypt, we have become slaves to technology. Cell phones, email, television, and the Internet are our twenty-first century taskmasters. Our technological tools allow 24-hour productivity and connectivity, give us more control ... and subtly enslave us to busyness itself.

Sabbath is about restraint, about intentionally *not* doing everything all the time just because we can. Setting aside a day of rest helps us reconnect with our Creator and find the peace of God that passes all understanding. The Sabbath is about letting go of the controls one day a week and letting God be God.

Musicians say that it is not the notes but the pauses between them that make the song. Similarly, the pauses between our workweeks add beauty and meaning to our lives. These Sabbath "stop days" turn the buzz of our busy lives into music.

REFLECTIONS ON REST

For years our family kept a weekly day of rest. Then I began preaching in churches around the country almost every Sunday and the trips out of town grew longer and more frequent. There was no longer a rhythm to my life, and I felt the strain—physically, emotionally, and spiritually.

I was regularly speaking about the importance of a day of rest each week and I began to ignore my own advice. In the midst of my self-made whirlwind, God sent me a reminder.

On a rare day home, I opened a letter. It was from a pastor whom I greatly respect. He was writing to encourage me, and to say how much he appreciated my work. At the end of the letter, he added a postscript: "Are you remembering to keep the Sabbath?"

Busted! After enjoying a weekly day of rest for years, somehow in the last few months I had given up my Sabbath.

In case I hadn't gotten the message, I received a second nudge. A few hours after I read the letter, I received a phone call from another pastor. I had spoken at his church some time ago, and he said that my discussion about the Sabbath had really struck a chord—not only for his congregation, but also for him personally. He told me that, for twenty years, he had suffered from depression. But now that he was religiously spending time in nature on his Sabbath, the depression had finally lifted. He was calling just to thank me.

Busted again!

The world gives us clocks; the Lord gives us time. There is more to life than how fast we can get through it. All of us have dozens of commitments, tasks, relationships, and other excuses pulling us away from enjoying the greatest gift of all—rest in God. For a few months, I neglected this gift; I hope that I never do again.

—Dr. Matthew Sleeth

SESSION NOTES: REST

As you watch the seventh session film, *Rest*, feel free to use the space below to jot down any notes, thoughts, and questions.

SESSION QUESTIONS: REST

1

Do you set aside a weekly day of rest? If not, what stops you? Do you have any traditions on your day of rest, or do you remember any from childhood?

"Remember the Sabbath day by keeping it holy."

—Exodus 20:8 NIV

2

Is working seven days a week a form of pride? How does coming to rest one day a week help us remember that the world doesn't revolve around, or depend on, us?

"Sabbath observance invites us to stop. It invites us to rest. It asks us to notice that while we rest the world continues without our help. It invites us to delight in the world's beauty and abundance."

—Wendell Berry, Foreword to *Living the Sabbath*

3

William Wilberforce, the nineteenth-century British states-man and abolitionist, wrote in his journal about his Sundays, "Blessed be to God for the day of rest and religious occupation wherein earthly things assume their true size."

How does observing a day of rest give God our full attention and help things "assume their true size"?

4

Dr. Sleeth compares the Hebrew people's bondage in Egypt to our bondage to technology and a 24/7 life. "People feel trapped by the technology that was meant to free them. It's not uncommon to hear someone say they cannot give up their technology even if they want to."

In what sense has technology become a taskmaster in your life? Give examples.

5

One of the most profound lines in the Bible is, "Be still and know that I am God." How does today's "I'm so busy" mantra distract us from God? Do you make time to "be still" on a regu-lar basis? If not, what changes in your routine would ensure that you make time for God?

6

Jesus says, "Come to me, all you who are weary and burdened, and I will give you rest. Take my yoke upon you and learn from me, for I am gentle and humble in heart, and you will find rest for your souls. For my yoke is easy and my burden is light."

How does Jesus' offer apply to our 24/7 lives? How is letting go and resting in Jesus a demonstration of faith and trust in His care and provision? What burdens could you place before Him today?

7

According to Dr. Sleeth, "A day of rest, or restraint, is needed now more than ever." What are some of the outcomes of not taking a day of rest? What would be some of the benefits, both personally and for society, if we took a regular day of rest? Explain the spiritual and environmental impact of working twenty-four hours a day, seven days a week. How can you encourage your church (or school or workplace) to take a weekly day of rest?

A CHANGED HEART = A CHANGED LIFE

Of all the steps our family has taken, honoring the Sabbath has given us the most joy. Until the last few decades, America still rested one day a week; a return to this custom could decrease pollution by 10 to 14 percent. Our family avoids driving on Sundays except to go to church, and we don't eat out or make purchases. Instead, we read, talk, listen to music, pray, and go for walks. When we miss a Sabbath day, we feel the negative impact throughout the week. When we honor the Sabbath, we honor our Creator with renewed faith and spirit.

Setting aside a day of rest must be intentional, but there's no real formula. Jesus says that it's the spirit of the law, not the letter, which matters. You may choose to abstain from certain activities on your Sabbath day — no shopping, no Internet, no emailing, no eating out. Or you may choose to spend your Sabbath reading aloud as a family, playing board games, or going on a walk. Once you start observing the Sabbath intentionally, you won't ever want to give it up. The Sabbath way of life can make every day a holy day.

How do you start? Preparing for the Sabbath takes forethought. If you don't want to shop on the Sabbath or you don't want to clean, you need to make sure you've done those things ahead of time. If you don't want work to interfere, you have to wrap things up in advance, let colleagues know that you don't answer calls or email on the Sabbath, and close up shop.

Our family cleans the house the day before the Sabbath; it takes about forty minutes for us to clear up clutter, dust, vacuum, scrub bathrooms, and clean the kitchen. We've been doing this for years. The reward is a relaxed home, with (almost) everything in its place.

Many people begin their Sabbath day at church in fellowship with God's people. However, if you are involved in running the nursery, worship team, choir, worship service, or Sunday school — if, in essence, you "work" at church on Sundays — consider taking an additional day for your day of rest.

Many families, unfortunately, end their Sabbath the moment they leave the church parking lot. Though it might be tempting to stop at the store on the way home from church, avoid running errands on the Sabbath. Our family tries not to engage in any commerce; God wants *all* people to have a chance to rest. It is often minimum-wage earners, today's "menservants and maid-servants," who have no choice but to work on weekends.

We need a day when we not only cease working, but also cease worrying about not working. Try putting away anything that reminds you of work. Shut down the computer. Don't answer email. Place your wallet, cell phone, PDA, and unpaid bills in a drawer. Close the door to your home office. Reminders of chores left undone, calls that need to be returned, and long to-do lists will interfere with the rest that God wants us to enjoy.

Consider including an hour of silence in your Sabbath day. To cease is to let God be God and enjoy his presence. One of our favorite Sabbath rituals is to take a Sabbath walk.

Most of all, Sabbath is about resting in God's love. The Sabbath is a time for loving our families and loving our friends. It's about embracing our church families, especially those who are struggling or feeling alone. It's about caring for strangers, inviting them into our homes and our lives. It's about loving God, loving His creation, and loving His living Word, including the commandment to rest. And it's about going into the week ahead, overflowing with Christ's love.

— Nancy Sleeth

Adapted with permission from *Go Green, Save Green: A Simple Guide to Saving Time, Money, and God's Green Earth* (Tyndale, 2009).

GOOD STEWARD ACTION PLAN: REST
Instructions

1. Pick two or more new actions from the suggested lists to commit to today and this year — or come up with your own way to honor the Sabbath.
2. Go to blessedearth.org and join our community of Good Stewards. Plus, you will find additional ideas for becoming a better steward of God's creation.
3. We will send you encouragements and help you stay on track with your goals. We're all in this together, so share your journey. Let us know what was easy, what was more difficult, and inspire others with your story!

TODAY, LORD, HELP ME TO:
Pick at least two of the following goals, or come up with your own actions.

○ Make a list of things to include and exclude on the Sabbath.
○ Talk with my family about when and how we want to celebrate the Sabbath.
○ Read Psalm 92.
○ Resolve not to run errands.
○ Select a family read-aloud book or devotional that I can share.

1. _____

2. _____

THIS YEAR, LORD, HELP ME TO:

Pick at least two of the following goals, or come up with your own actions.

O Clean the house before the Sabbath.

O Get all my errands done before the Sabbath.

O Take off my watch or put away my cell phone and remove all reminders of work on my day of rest.

O Turn off my computer and keep it off all day.

O Use the answering machine to screen calls or voicemail to save calls.

O Encourage my family to rest.

O Avoid driving on my day of rest, except to church.

O Avoid eating out and buying things on the Sabbath.

O Observe some quiet time on the Sabbath.

O Read Psalms 23, 24, 29, 93, 126, and 148.

1. _____

2. _____

Adapted with permission from *Go Green, Save Green: A Simple Guide to Saving Time, Money, and God's Green Earth*, by Nancy Sleeth (Tyndale, 2009).

"I was raised in a conservative Jewish home. Every Friday night, we lit the candles, said a blessing over the bread and wine, and shared a Sabbath meal. We frequently added a leaf to the table to make room for family friends. Now, as a Christian family, we incorporate a few of these Hebrew prayers and Sabbath observances. It delights me to remember that Jesus, Mary, and Joseph observed similar traditions in their home."

—Nancy Sleeth

Session 8

WORK

SESSION SUMMARY

> *"Always give yourselves fully to the work of the Lord, because you know that your labor in the Lord is not in vain."*
>
> — 1 Corinthians 15:58 NIV

A majority of our life is spent at work. The availability of work, and the health and opportunity to do work are blessings. Work itself is a good thing; God created us to work.

Humanity's first work assignment is found in the second chapter of Genesis; we are told to be gardeners — men and women together, protecting and tending the earth. This mandate applies whether we're tilling the soil or shopping in the grocery store.

God's intent for humankind to care for the planet and all its creatures doesn't have an expiration date. It didn't run out at the fall or at the cross; God's instructions for Adam and Eve stretch through time to our day and age — and beyond.

All of us were meant to be caretakers. It is the work of our lives, but what does it mean to be stewards of the earth at a computer, on the construction site, or down at the plant? Few of us are shepherds, farmers, or gardeners by profession.

Irrespective of our particular occupation, God is calling *all* of us to take better care of the planet. We must examine our work in light of the gifts we have been given and the biblical call to care for the earth. As a result of this self-examination, some of us may feel called to new work; most of us will find new ways of getting to and from work, purchasing materials, delivering goods and services, and performing tasks in ways that better demonstrate our love for God and what He's made. No activity is exempt; nearly every task can be made "greener." This is not something we can delegate. It will require work.

However, this work is best done together. Workplaces are communities where we can share our unique gifts and talents in service of God to benefit others. We can create a ripple effect and show what Christians are *for*, serving with a joyful attitude as caretakers of God's green earth.

REFLECTIONS ON WORK

For seven years after I graduated from high school, I worked as a carpenter. One of my favorite memories as a builder was framing up houses in the fall. The air was crisp and clear, my body was still strong and capable of working hard, and there was something that felt good about working with other people.

At the end of each day we would put away our tools and survey the progress we had made. While the task of sawing each individual rafter to the right length and angle might seem mundane, seeing entire walls, ceilings, and roofs emerge in what used to be open air is nothing short of miraculous. It's rewarding to build something in the place of nothing; we can only imagine how God must have enjoyed the process of creating a home for all His creatures — this remarkably diverse planet we call Earth.

In the beginning, after creating the earth and waters and skies, God placed Adam in the Garden of Eden. Adam had only one boss, and this boss gave Adam a pretty interesting assignment: God told Adam to tend and protect the garden.

As caretaker of the entire earth, Adam was responsible for helping new things grow and flourish. He was steward of all creation. And in those first days, Adam was 100 percent connected with God in his every effort. This is how God intended work to be: done in humility, in service of Him.

Humanity has strayed from this original mandate to tend and protect: instead, our desire for comfort and convenience has caused much harm to the planet. Yet physical work can provide health and meaning to our lives. While the disciples sailed, Jesus walked across the Sea of Galilee to meet them. He picked grain. He washed his disciples' feet. Work was not beneath him. He thought no physical labor was undignified. The washing of feet is a sign that God is willing to stoop low and to work to save us. Shouldn't we be willing to work with all our hearts, minds, souls, and strength to help save His creation?

— Dr. Matthew Sleeth

SESSION NOTES: WORK

As you watch the eighth session film, *Work*, use the space below to jot down notes, thoughts, and questions.

SESSION QUESTIONS: WORK

1

From the very beginning, the Bible teaches us that work is a good activity. Why has work gotten a bad reputation? Do we work just to buy things, or does work have other value besides a paycheck?

2

How is work a blessing? How does too much or too little work affect our mental, physical, emotional, and spiritual health?

"The availability of work, and the health and opportunity to do work, are blessings."

—Dr. Matthew Sleeth

3

Dr. Sleeth says, "We were all meant to be gardeners. It is the work of our lives. But what does it mean to be gardeners at a computer, in a cubicle, on the construction site, or down at the plant?"

How would you answer that question? How do you—or can you—better care for and protect the parts of God's creation entrusted to your care?

4

What qualities make work "godly"? Are these qualities found in your current work at home or the office? Do you perceive your daily work as service to God?

"The idea that the service to God should have only to do with a church altar, singing, reading, sacrifice, and the like is without doubt but the worst trick of the devil. How could the devil have led us more effectively astray than by the narrow conception that service to God takes place only in a church and by the works done therein.... The whole world could abound with the services to the Lord ... not only in churches but also in the home, kitchen, workshop, field."

—Martin Luther (1483-1546)

5

Dr. Sleeth compares Paul and Zacchaeus and the effect of their conversion experiences on their line of work. For Paul, his conversion resulted in a complete career change. In Zacchaeus' case, his occupation didn't change, but how he performed his work changed radically. How about you? Have you felt a call from God to change your work? If so, in what direction do you feel God leading? How does knowing and following Jesus affect how you do your work?

6

Dr. Sleeth states: "Irrespective of your particular job, God is calling all of us to take better care of the planet. This is not something we can delegate.... There's no activity that a business is involved in that can't be made greener."

What are some ways you can modify your work activities—and the activities of your business, company, or organization—to better care for creation? Give examples.

A CHANGED HEART = A CHANGED LIFE

My first real job after college was as a technical writer at a Department of Energy research facility. My office was in a trailer that had been salvaged from the 1977 Johnstown, Pennsylvania, flood. The orange carpet was perpetually damp and the air had a distinctive, old-mold smell.

Six months later I was promoted to the administrative offices — a bunch of newly manufactured trailers linked together to create one large maze of cubicles. If you've ever gotten a whiff of a "new car smell," multiply that tenfold and you'll have a sense of the air we inhaled eight hours a day. At twenty-one, I wasn't particularly concerned about the long-term health consequences of indoor air pollution or the number of trees we used editing multiple drafts of long bureaucratic reports — I was just grateful to have a job that paid the bills.

My colleagues were mostly engineers, trying to find ways of burning fossil fuels — particularly coal — more cleanly and efficiently. Three decades later, scientists and engineers are still searching for the holy grail of "clean coal" (a term many now consider an oxymoron). Despite good intentions, my work at the research facility probably did more environmental harm than good — using lots of resources with little or no benefit to the planet.

When I switched from technical writing to teaching English, the results of my work seemed more straightforward. It wasn't until I taught at the boarding school, however, that my advocacy for health, environmental, and money-saving changes went into high gear. By then, Matthew had left medicine, and we had significantly downscaled our lifestyle. After successfully implementing so many changes at home, I now felt it was time to help lighten the footprint of my workplace.

During my first contract meeting with my boss, I explained that taking care of the planet was my passion. He politely told me that it was not his.

It took a few years, but — despite some initial resistance — the workplace gradually became greener: we began to use recycled paper in all copiers and offices; set double-sided printing as the default in printers; installed LED bulbs in exit signs; added motion detectors for interior lighting; installed dimmers in rooms with natural light; added Dumpster-sized recycling receptacles for paper, glass, plastics, and metal; greatly reduced the use of Styrofoam in the cafeteria; and began composting food waste.

The key to success was working with the system — and forming a "green team" — to make the workplace healthier, more environmentally responsible, and more cost-effective.

The typical office worker uses a quarter of a ton (500 pounds) of materials in a year, including ten thousand pieces of copy paper.

With a little imagination, any field can be made more green: office workers can arrange a rideshare board, hairdressers can compost hair clippings, landscapers can use native plants, house cleaners can switch to natural cleaning products, restaurants can purchase locally grown food. Starting a green task force that recommends ways to save the company money while saving the earth and creating a healthier work environment will result in a win-win-win bottom line.

Can it be challenging to initiate changes at work? Yes. Will you face obstacles? Definitely. The great thing about changes in the workplace is that they have the potential to make a big difference. Not only can you reduce the environmental impact of the entire company, but your example can also influence coworkers' behavior at home.

When colleagues ask why you are going green, don't hesitate to say that your faith is a primary motivation. By adopting good stewardship practices, you are sharing your love of the Creator — and becoming a living testimony through your behavior. Think of creation care as a mission field — an opportunity for us to grow ever closer to the example set by Jesus — and a tangible way to share His perfect love with those who have fewer resources than we do.

— Nancy Sleeth

Adapted with permission from Go Green, Save Green: A Simple Guide to Saving Time, Money, and God's Green Earth (Tyndale, 2009).

GOOD STEWARD ACTION PLAN: WORK
Instructions

1. Pick two or more new actions from the suggested lists to commit to today and this year — or come up with your own ideas for serving God and caring for the earth through your work.
2. Go to blessedearth.org and join our community of Good Stewards. Explore the website to find additional ideas for saving energy and becoming a better steward of God's creation.
3. We will send you encouragement throughout the year and help you stay on track with your goals. As God's fellow workers, we're all in this together, so share your journey. Let us know what was easy, what was more difficult, and inspire others with your story!

TODAY, LORD, HELP ME TO:
Pick at least two of the following goals, or come up with your own actions.

O Pray that my work habits would reflect Christ's love for people and creation.

O Activate my computer's standby mode setting.

O Set my printer's default setting to double-sided printing.

O Use draft mode for printing when documents aren't yet final.

O Bring my own coffee mug to work instead of using disposable cups.

O Turn off my computer, printer, and peripherals when I leave work for the day.

O Turn off the lights when I leave my workspace; work under natural light when possible.

1. _____

2. _____

THIS YEAR, LORD, HELP ME TO:

Pick at least two of the following goals, or come up with your own actions.

- ○ Ask my employer about the possibility of telecommuting one day a week or working a four-day week.
- ○ Carpool with someone who lives and works near me; use public transportation, walk, or bike to work when possible.
- ○ Print documents only when necessary.
- ○ Reuse envelopes and packaging products in the office.
- ○ Take the stairs instead of the elevator.
- ○ Give up two restaurant or cafeteria lunches; bring a lunch from home in reusable containers instead.
- ○ Investigate ink cartridge and e-waste recycling opportunities.
- ○ Set up a recycling box and bring home the recyclables myself if there is no recycling program at work.

1. _____

2. _____

"I believe that God wants us to live in tension, constantly working to make decisions that bring us closer to Him. Anybody could point at me and say 'hypocrite' regarding many aspects of my work and home life. One area that we currently struggle with is transportation. I need to travel to churches to share our message, and try to do it in the most environmentally responsible way—grouping events geographically, driving in an efficient car, carpooling, etc. But it would be better if I did not have to travel at all.... We are all on this creation care journey together. If we can do a little more each year, we're on the right path."

—Matthew Sleeth

Adapted with permission from *Go Green, Save Green: A Simple Guide to Saving Time, Money, and God's Green Earth*, by Nancy Sleeth (Tyndale, 2009) and www.blessedearth.org.

Session 9

GIVE

SESSION SUMMARY

"It is more blessed to give than to receive."
— Acts 20:35 NIV

When we take only what we need, we often find that we have far more resources at our disposal than we can consume for ourselves. When we steward our time and work to provide for our needs, taking what we need for today and trusting God with tomorrow, most of us have an abundance left over. And we're faced with a choice: store up treasure for ourselves here on earth ... or give it away.

The first story of giving in the Bible is that of Cain and Abel. These are the sons of Adam and Eve. Abel brings the very best of what he has as an offering to God. In contrast, Cain holds back. And as a result, sin pours into his life, damaging his relationship with God and his brother.

Right from the start we are taught something fundamental about the human heart: lack of generosity keeps us from God.

It doesn't matter if this is in church, at work, or at home: holding back is wrong. It's one of the greatest affronts to the spirit of God. Give without thinking, give the best, and you're on the right track. The most winsome trait of a follower of Christ is generosity.

If we start with the premise that our God is a generous God, a God who gives without thought of balancing accounts, then how should we act if we are made in God's image and called to imitate Him?

Scripture is clear: hoarding is bad; giving is good—for us, for our neighbors, and for God's green earth.

REFLECTIONS ON GIVE

Two of my dearest friends, Geoff and Sherry, bought a house in the poorest section of Lexington, Kentucky. They are two of the most generous people I know, living out their love of Christ through daily acts of kindness toward the people in their community.

They've started an urban garden, served on the low-income housing board, and remained extremely active in the neighborhood association. Geoff regularly helps with refugees who come to Lexington from war-torn countries and Sherry is working to start an urban orchard and outdoor classroom.

Both are deeply devoted to their neighbors. Hospitality is a top priority in their home, and they nearly always have at least one non-family member living with them. People stop by for dinner and stay for a month. They are listed as the next of kin for several elderly neighbors and have been called to the hospital in the middle of the night to help make major life decisions. Neighbors knock on their door and unload their troubled lives.

Sherry recently told me about a severely mentally challenged man who shows up at their door fairly regularly, often before dawn. He thinks he is the godfather of their six-year-old son, and Geoff and Sherry treat him as if he really is Isaac's godfather, inviting him in for a cup of coffee before the birds are even awake.

I know we are not supposed to envy, but I do. I envy the way they dare to care, as our Lord Jesus did, for those who have been marginalized and abandoned.

Geoff and Sherry have lived for the last decade on a modest income, but they are rich beyond measure. I have seen them share their income with a young couple who had even less than they did. Their selfless, joyous generosity has taught me much about God's economy, where it truly is better to give than receive.

— Nancy Sleeth

Adapted with permission from *Go Green, Save Green: A Simple Guide to Saving Time, Money, and God's Green Earth* (Tyndale, 2009).

SESSION NOTES: GIVE

As you watch the ninth session film, *Give*, use the space below to jot down notes, thoughts, and questions.

SESSION QUESTIONS: GIVE

1

What do you do with the first fruits of your labor? Do you pay the bills first, and then give, or give first and then pay the bills?

"After we have rested, then comes work. And after we have worked, we have the fruits of our labor. This can literally be fruits or vegetables, but more often the harvest is money or expertise."

— Dr. Matthew Sleeth

2

Dr. Sleeth says, "Our lack of generosity keeps us from God. It doesn't matter if this is in church, or at work, or at home. Holding back is wrong. It's one of the greatest affronts to the spirit of God."

In what sense does a lack of generosity keep us from God? Why is it wrong? How is it an "affront" to God?

3

Dr. Sleeth asks, "If we start with the premise that our God is a generous God, a God who gives without thought of balancing accounts—then how should we act if we are made in God's image?" In Ephesians, we're specifically called to be "imitators of God." Do your giving habits reflect God's—His extravagant generosity? If not, what is holding you back?

4

How do you define your needs? How has God demonstrated His faithfulness to provide for you? What percent of your money do you believe God is calling you to give toward helping others? How do you determine the "right amount" to give?

"In the Old Testament, we learn about the tithe, or the giving of 10 percent to help the widow, the orphan, the refugee, and the work of the church. But in our land of plenty, what is the right amount to give away today? How do we separate our wants from our needs?"

—Dr. Matthew Sleeth

5

Jesus teaches that the way we spend our resources serves as a reflection of our hearts. God sees our true motivations. He knows that if our hearts are focused on storing treasures in heaven, we won't worry about the things we "want" on this earth. When we properly use the resources God has given us, we'll be more concerned with loving Him, loving His creation, and loving our neighbors instead of our own comfort on earth — and we'll lead both spiritual and environmentally sustainable lives. Right now, today, you are an investor. Where are you investing? How do your spending habits reveal the priorities of your heart?

"Do not store up for yourselves treasures on earth, where moths and vermin destroy, and where thieves break in and steal. But store up for yourselves treasures in heaven, where moths and vermin do not destroy, and where thieves do not break in and steal. For where your treasure is, there your heart will be also."

— Matthew 6:19 – 21 NIV

6 Dr. Sleeth observes, "Money is not the only valuable thing that we can give away. One area that costs nothing but we are all too often stingy with is encouragement and compliments." When was the last time you gave a compliment or sent a note of encouragement? Name some specific ways you can be more generous with positive words.

7 Tending and protecting the planet requires sacrifice. Explain how living more simply, taking less for ourselves, and conserving resources is a form of giving. In what sense are recycling, adjusting the thermostat, and using public transportation acts of sacrificial giving? In what ways are you giving sacrificially? How could you give more? How can living this way bring us closer to Christ's generous example?

A CHANGED HEART = A CHANGED LIFE

One way our family has learned to give is by making "our" home a center for mission and ministry. Our first mission was to recycle.

▶ **Four out of every five pieces of junk mail are not recycled. Junk mail fills 340,000 garbage trucks a year, all bound for landfills.**

The paper in these mountains of un-asked-for mail comes from trees, the dyes are chemicals, and the dioxin created in the papermaking process contaminates our freshwater supplies so that I can't eat a fish from the river that runs by our house without risking cancer. Recycling aluminum cans, for example, helps prevent mountains from being leveled and prevents water supplies from being contaminated. Recycling is a simple way for my family to give back to global neighbors.

Another way our family decided to give is by not buying products made from rainforest timber. How does refraining from buying a teak chair constitute "giving"? As the demand for disposable chopsticks and teak furniture grows, the trees in the third world are cut down, the topsoil washes away, the streams dry up, and impoverished villagers flee to cities where childhood prostitution, exploitation, gangs, violence, and corruption are the norm.

▶ **Not using throwaway chopsticks can keep an eight-year-old out of a brothel in Indonesia.**

Our "best buys" are simply to forgo a purchase altogether. In general, we've come to realize that if we've lived without it for the first twenty-five years of our marriage, we can probably do without it forever. Buying less is not only good for the planet, it frees up money for us to give to others.

Sometimes, however, it's worth paying more. If the product is cheaply made and might easily break, it represents another kind of waste. Also, unbeknownst to most Americans, one consequence of our demand for ever-lower prices is that many companies now use underpaid labor to keep costs down in a competitive market. As followers of Jesus, it's worth paying a premium for Fair Trade certified products to ensure the well-being of our global neighbors.

These are simple "sacrifices" to make. When I read Butler's *Lives of Martyrs*, I marvel. Those heroes of God were stabbed, mauled, impaled, dismembered, and burned as a witness to their love of Jesus. Their sacrifice did not drive others away from Christ but toward him. Roman guards in charge of these martyrs were converted on the spot and gave up their own lives.

Now, hanging clothing on the line, giving up plastic wrap, and changing the light bulbs are hardly the equivalent of being burned alive as a human torch to light up one of Nero's parties. But even today, people, like the Roman guards, are drawn to anyone who believes in something enough to change his lifestyle.

Our new house has no clothes dryer, garbage disposal, or garage, but it's a place of sharing and prayer. We happily have several dozen people into our house for neighborhood pot-luck dinners, student cookouts, and faith groups. I do not think that anyone can say what the "right" size house is; compared to homes I have visited on medical missions in Honduras, our current house is indefensibly large. We still live better than nearly everyone else on the planet, and we are looking to downsize again. Each time we divest ourselves of possessions, we have fewer earthly things that bind us.

None of these changes we've made will earn us entrance into heaven, but they do two important things for our souls: they connect us with the family of humanity around the globe, and, more importantly, they bring us closer to the heart of God. If He asks us to give up everything we have and follow Him, as He asked the rich young ruler, I now know with certainty that each member of my family would gladly do so. This lack of attachment to material things brings us priceless freedom to give without thinking whenever we hear God's call.

—Dr. Matthew Sleeth

Adapted with permission from *Serving God, Saving the Planet* (Zondervan, 2007).

GOOD STEWARD ACTION PLAN: GIVE
Instructions

1. Pick two or more new actions from the suggested lists to commit to today and this year — or come up with your own way to imitate the generosity of our gracious God.
2. Go to blessedearth.org and join our community of Good Stewards. Explore the website to find additional ideas for saving energy and becoming a better steward of God's creation.
3. We will send you encouragements throughout the year and help you stay on track with your goals. As followers of Christ, we're all in this together, so share your journey. Let us know what was easy, what was difficult, and inspire others with your story!

TODAY, LORD, HELP ME TO:
Pick at least two of the following goals, or come up with your own actions.

O Memorize one or more Bible verses about giving, such as 2 Corinthians 9:7 or 1 John 3:17.
O Pick up trash in my neighborhood.
O Compliment or encourage someone who goes out of the way to care for God's creation.
O Donate all pocket change.
O Gather up a bag of nonperishable food to drop off at a food pantry.
O Plant trees by donating to Floresta, Eden Reforestation Project, or Heifer International.

1. _____

2. _____

THIS YEAR, LORD, HELP ME TO:

Pick at least two of the following goals, or come up with your own actions.

○ Bring Fair Trade coffee to work; volunteer to wash coffee mugs.

○ Take someone to lunch at a restaurant that uses local or organic foods.

○ Offer to run errands for someone when I'm going out.

○ Use public transportation.

○ Share produce from my garden or extra baked goods with a neighbor.

○ Shop at a local business instead of a chain store, or shop at the farmers' market.

○ If I have more than I need (TVs, DVD players, computers, tools), give them away so someone can use them NOW, not someday.

○ Perform an act of kindness for someone in my neighborhood (babysit so the parents can have a date; shovel a sidewalk).

○ Walk or bike distances of less than two miles.

○ Invite a family in my neighborhood over for dinner.

○ Borrow something from a neighbor instead of buying it.

1. _____

2. _____

"We have one friend who hosts neighborhood gatherings in her backyard the first Sunday of each month. Her house is one of the smallest in the neighborhood, but she and her husband have a big heart for hospitality. The gatherings keep getting bigger, as neighbors invite other neighbors. Over the last year, these Sunday potlucks have become a central part of their family ministry, and a focal point for neighborly sharing. From friends like this, I have learned not to wait for someone else to initiate community activities; if you plan it, they will come."

— Nancy Sleeth

Session 10

SHARE

SESSION SUMMARY

*"Love one another. As I have loved you, so you
must love one another. By this everyone will know
you are my disciples, if you love one another."*
— John 13:34 - 35 NIV

The first-century church was a happening church — a foretaste
of heaven. All the believers met together constantly, selling their
possessions and sharing everything with those in need. They
worshiped together, sharing meals with great joy and generosity.
All during this time people were praising God and enjoying each
other's company. And each day new members were added to
their gatherings.

It's quite a picture — people who see church not as a building
but as a way of life. What a far cry from our concept of church
today! As a society we long for community; we long for a sense
of belonging. So how did we get from church as described in
the Bible where joyful generosity was the norm to where we are
today?

Today, we live in a country that makes up just 5 percent of
the world's population, and yet we use 25 percent of the world's
energy. We use roughly half the world's paper. Is it possible to
conserve resources, and at the same time build fellowship? Yes!

The trick is to be more like the first-century church. More simply, the trick is to be more like Jesus.

I believe part of the reason we buy so much and we own so much is because it's easier to remain isolated and independent than to share. As Americans, we not only define ourselves by the things we own, but we take pride in not having to ask for anything. Individualism and independence are some of our culture's supreme values. By sharing and practicing hospitality, we return to "church" as God intended it to be.

Church is a verb — a dynamic, active community engaged in loving service — not a static noun. Love one another, and by this, all of humanity will know you follow Jesus.

REFLECTIONS ON SHARE

Sharing is about generosity, and generosity is the engine of the church. In his book Life Together, *Dietrich Bonhoeffer — the brilliant German theologian who died a martyr in a Nazi concentration camp — talks about the grace that God affords us by allowing us to live in community with fellow believers. Bonhoeffer suggests that one of the greatest blessings one can have is life together.*

As the first-century church discovered, life together is not always easy. When you "do church," there will be friction and controversy. We have all been raised in an environment of hyper individuality and must actively practice the skills that allow us to live together.

God's church, as His bride and the body of Christ, is meant to be a community of people who care for one another and serve as the hands and feet of Jesus in the world. The church community is a natural place to give, borrow, and lend. Scripture is explicit about the need to share: "[D]o not refuse anyone who wants to borrow from you" (Matthew 5:42).

Church also offers opportunities for extending hospitality. I did not grow up in a home that offered much in the way of hospitality, and I have learned much from those who open their homes to me — and from my wife, Nancy. She seems to have a natural gift for making people comfortable. Over a recent week we had thirty-nine people over for dinner in five different groups. Hospitality is not always easy, but it's a great way to build community.

One of the groups was comprised of neighbors — many of whom are training to become pastors. We have started to work together in an intentional way to share tools, a garden, and automobiles. No neighborhood need own more than one chainsaw, power saw, copy of a particular movie, or extension ladder.

God owns the earth, and everything on it. By learning to work cooperatively, the church honors God, our ever-gracious Host.

— Dr. Matthew Sleeth

Adapted with permission from *The Gospel According to the Earth: Why the Good Book Is a Green Book* (HarperOne, 2010).

SESSION NOTES: SHARE

As you watch the tenth session film, *Share*, use the space below to jot down notes, thoughts, and questions.

SESSION QUESTIONS: SHARE

1

Dr. Sleeth, paraphrasing the book of Acts, describes the first-century church as follows: "All the believers met together constantly. They sold their possessions and shared everything with those in need. They worshiped together each day, and they met in homes for the Lord's Supper. They shared their meals with great joy and generosity. All during this time people were praising God and enjoying each other's company. And each day new members were added to the group that was being saved."

How is this description of the first-century church different from the church today? In what sense has the church become a building rather than a way of life?

2

In his book, *The Great Divorce*, C. S. Lewis depicts hell as a place of infinite resources. How can unlimited resources—what most would consider a blessing—lead to undesirable behaviors and outcomes? Give examples.

3

How does the first-century church differ from our twenty-first century church? How does our culture's focus on wealth and independence pull us away from interdependence and sharing?

"As a society we long for community. We long for a feeling of belonging."
— Dr. Matthew Sleeth

4

Jesus tells us in Luke 12, "From everyone who has been given much, much will be demanded; and from the one who has been entrusted with much, much more will be asked." God shares with us that we might share with others. How does this understanding affect the way you hold on to, let go of, and use the gifts — material goods and personal talents and passions — that He's given to you? Why do you think God has entrusted you with the good things in your life?

5

Dr. Sleeth observes: "Just as hard as it is to give, it's sometimes even harder to receive." In what sense can asking for or accepting the generosity and hospitality of others be a humbling experience?

6 How can the church foster "love for the Creator and for the Creator's garden"? How can the church help us "turn aside from greed and materialism" and pursue a "right relationship with God, neighbor, and earth"?

"If we are ever able to stop destroying our environment, it will be because person by person we decide, by God's grace, to turn aside from greed and materialism. It will be because we learn that joy and fulfillment come through right relationship with God, neighbor, and earth, not an ever-escalating demand for more and more material consumption. Nowhere is that more possible than in local congregations that combine prayer and action, worship and analysis, deep personal love for the Creator and for the Creator's garden."

—Dr. Ronald Sider, Professor of Theology and Society, Eastern Baptist Theological Seminary

7 Is your church "green"? What responsibility do you have as an individual member of the body of Christ to be a better steward of creation? What actions are more easily done together? How can you help your church reclaim its God-given responsibility to care for the earth?

"The adoption of statements on the environment by church councils and assemblies is important. But unless every local congregation actually carries out sound environmental practices in its buildings and in the homes of the members, these statements are worthless. Care of the earth—our mandate from the Creator—is the responsibility of us all."

—The Reverend Dr. Herbert W. Chilstrom (b. 1931), Bishop, Evangelical Lutheran Church in America

A CHANGED HEART = A CHANGED LIFE

A few years ago, Matthew was asked to preach at the church where he grew up. As a result, the church formed five book groups to study *Serving God, Saving the Planet*, using the discussion guide to apply stewardship principles to their daily lives at home, work, and church. Out of these book studies, an ongoing creation care group was formed. The group recommended energy-saving actions throughout the church, including changing lightbulbs, making recycling bins readily available, and using nondisposable dishes.

One church member bought a dozen cases of lightbulbs to share at cost. They sold out immediately, with requests for more bulbs at the next service. The pastor and creation care group also encouraged their building committee to hire a green architect for their new addition. Once the creation care group got going, God opened doors they never dreamed of!

Jesus tells us in Matthew 7 to take the plank out of our own eye before worrying about the speck in someone else's. As sons and daughters of God, we need to clean up our own churchyards first. The changes we make at church show the outside world that we honor the Lord not only in what we say but also in what we do.

D. L. Moody once said, "There are many of us that are willing to do great things for the Lord, but few of us are willing to do the little things." Seemingly small acts, like recycling used announcements, really *do* make a difference. Following are some ideas for getting started:

1. Conduct an energy audit, either through your local utility or a performance contractor. Many church buildings can be made more efficient.

2. Change the lighting in the church to be more energy-efficient.

3. Recycle church bulletins. Encourage people to share bulletins, and reduce the size of the bulletin to fewer pages. Print them on recycled paper.
4. Purchase organic, Fair Trade coffee. Use ceramic mugs instead of disposable cups.
5. Organize a church garden. Soup kitchens, homeless shelters, and local after-school programs will welcome your fresh produce. A church garden is also a great way to engage people who normally don't go to church but are interested in gardening or community service.
6. Start an exchange program. Set up a bulletin board for people to post items they need and items they want to give away. Consider starting a "library" for tools and toys, in addition to books, magazines, and videos.
7. Start a book study or small group on God-centered environmentalism and discuss how group members can reduce their impact on ecosystems.
8. Hold prayer meetings for people affected by environmental changes and natural disasters. Pray for wisdom to know how to help and the strength to carry out God's will.
9. Plant trees native to your region.
10. Organize car pools to and from church. If you have many people coming from one area (such as college students or senior citizens), arrange for a van or bus to take them all to church instead of them driving separately.
11. Share the church building with other organizations. Multiple church congregations can share one church building on Saturdays and Sundays. Soup kitchens and community groups can use the building during the week.
12. Turn off electronic devices in the church when they're not in use.

13. Reduce waste. Set up recycling bins in the church kitchen and throughout the building. Place boxes for cans, plastic, and paper, and bring them to the recycling center on a regular basis.

14. Clean green. Make sure that the cleaning products used at the church are not harmful for the environment and contain no phosphates.

15. Curb clutter. Hold a church yard sale. The fewer things we have, the less distraction in our lives and the more time we have to spend with God. Donate the money raised to church outreach, missions, and worthy charities.

Finally, love one another, for by this the world will know you are Christ's disciples. "Religion that God our Father accepts as pure and faultless is this: to look after orphans and widows in their distress and to keep oneself from being polluted by the world" (James 1:27 NIV). "The only thing that counts is faith expressing itself through love" (Galatians 5:6 NIV).

— Nancy Sleeth

Adapted with permission from *Go Green, Save Green: A Simple Guide to Saving Time, Money, and God's Green Earth* (Tyndale, 2009).

GOOD STEWARD ACTION PLAN: SHARE
Instructions

1. Pick two or more new actions from the suggested lists to commit to today and this year — or come up with your own way to build a Christlike community.
2. Go to blessedearth.org and join our community of Good Stewards. Explore the website to find additional ideas for saving energy and becoming a better steward of God's creation.
3. We will send you encouragements throughout the year and help you stay on track with your goals. As the body of Christ, we're all in this together, so share your journey. Let us know what was easy, what was difficult, and inspire others with your story!

TODAY, LORD, HELP ME TO:
Pick at least two of the following goals, or come up with your own actions.

O Look online to learn about my church's or denomination's stance on earth stewardship.

O Make a list of people who might be interested in forming a creation care group at my church.

O Visit web resources related to environmentally sustainable churches and download one of the energy-saving guides:
   - www.blessedearth.org
   - www.creationcare.org
   - www.earthministry.org
   - www.energystar.gov
   - www.theregenerationproject.org
   - www.webofcreation.org

1. _____

2. _____

THIS YEAR, LORD, HELP ME TO:
Pick at least two of the following goals, or come up with your own actions.

○ Give someone a ride to church to reduce pollution.

○ Talk to friends about how we can help our church be a better steward.

○ Walk around the church building and take notes on ways the church could use less resources.

○ Encourage my church to conduct an energy audit.

○ Make a list of low- or no-cost changes my church community could make to become better stewards.

○ See if my church serves Fair Trade coffee; if they don't, research local Fair Trade options and make the switch.

○ Pray for people affected by environmental degradation around the world.

○ Ask my pastor to preach a sermon or series on creation care or invite a guest speaker.

○ Talk to the facilities manager at my church about recycling options.

○ Ask custodial staff to switch to eco-friendly cleaning products.

1. _____

2. _____

"New monastic groups and home churches are springing up throughout the country. I believe that these home churches are a vital way to fill our longing for community life. In a similar way, within medium sized churches and mega-churches, small groups act as communities within communities, providing a way to belong, to worship, and to share in the context of an often impersonal world."
— Dr. Matthew Sleeth

TEACH

SESSION SUMMARY

> *"Teach them to their children, so the next generation might know them—even the children not yet born—and they in turn will teach their own children."*
>
> **—Psalm 78:5-6 NLT**

Most people have never heard a sermon on Genesis 2:15, God's first job assignment for humanity—the command to tend and protect the earth. They haven't been taught why the Bible says not to cut a fruit tree even in war, or why we are instructed not to muddy the waters. Yet teaching about what the Bible teaches us about caring for the earth and all living things is both a responsibility and a privilege.

How do we teach these lessons? We look to the methods of the ultimate Teacher, Jesus. Sometimes He answers questions with questions. Sometimes He answers directly, like He did when asked how to pray: Pray the Lord's Prayer.

During His ministry on earth, Jesus teaches through stories, rebuke, and encouragement. But perhaps the best way to teach is through example. Too often we want to be the judge and the jury for God, but what Christ is asking us to do is be the witness.

Christ's most memorable lessons are those taught by His life. Jesus made a sacrifice two thousand years ago to pay for my sins, and your sins — the sins of yesterday, today, tomorrow, and forever. And in doing so, He taught us something profound about time: What we do now — even the sacrifices we make — matter for generations to come.

My prayer is that when someone looks at you, they see someone who is humble and meek and willing to sacrifice for the next generation in the same way Christ sacrificed for you.

REFLECTIONS ON TEACH

I know that teachers are not supposed to have favorites, but Josh was a very special boy. At age five, he was extremely inquisitive, honest, and affectionate. He also was obsessed with war. One day, when Josh had just finished drawing yet another exquisitely detailed sword and shield, I asked about this obsession.

Josh was quiet for a full two minutes. A thoughtful boy, he clearly wanted to give me a truthful answer. Finally, he looked me straight in the eyes and replied, "Mrs. Sleeth, it's because boys are boys and girls are girls." A simple yet profound insight for a five-year-old!

I recently finished reading The Idiot by the Russian novelist Fyodor Dostoevsky. His main character, the Christlike hero Prince Myshkin, has a special relationship with children, just as Jesus did. Young children love the Prince because he is honest and never tries to deceive them. Further, Myshkin has found, as I did with Josh, that "a child can give exceedingly good advice even in the most difficult case."

I will never forget what I learned from Josh about the differences between boys and girls, and I will never forget the lessons my students taught me each time we went outdoors: turn your face up to the first flakes of snow; watch a butterfly shake its wings dry; lie on your back and imagine shapes in the clouds.

Though we can share knowledge with children, they can teach us something even more valuable: wonderment. Children instinctively understand that nature is precious — more valuable than anything humans can make. They live in the joy of the eternal present, neither dwelling on the past nor fretting about the future.

As adults, we must "train up a child in the way he should go," but at the same time be humble and patient enough to receive

instruction, for the "kingdom of heaven belongs to such as these."
When it comes to the environment, perhaps the best gift my stu-
dents gave me was hope.

— Nancy Sleeth

Adapted with permission from Go Green, Save Green: A Simple Guide to
Saving Time, Money, and God's Green Earth (Tyndale, 2009).

SESSION NOTES: TEACH

As you watch the eleventh session film, *Teach*, use the space below to jot down notes, thoughts, and questions.

SESSION QUESTIONS: TEACH

1

What steps has your church taken to pass along a love and respect for God's creation?

"Teaching about Genesis 2:15 and the hundreds of other green passages in the Bible is a responsibility. We are to pass along the wisdom of the ages to our children, and to their children. Teaching is a biblical calling."

—Dr. Matthew Sleeth

2

Dr. Sleeth says, "We want to be the judge and the jury for God, but what Christ is asking us to do is be the witness." How can you be the "witness" for God as you teach about caring for creation? Name some actions you could take that would speak louder than words.

3 ─────────────────────────────

Dr. Sleeth admits, "One of my favorite ways of being taught is by being encouraged. I respond so much better to encouragement than discouragement! Jesus was certainly good at encouraging ... we need to do the same, whether we're teaching somebody Bible lessons or about recycling." Who can you encourage today? What can you do to affirm someone's efforts to care for creation?

4 ─────────────────────────────

Dr. Sleeth suggests, "Saying 'turn off the water' to kids is one thing, but showing them three gallons of water that's wasted while brushing their teeth is quite another." Can you think of other examples of how we can teach about the importance of caring for God's creation through hands-on experience?

5

In what sense does nature "speak with the voice of God"? What will we hear if we listen? What can nature teach us about God's provision, contentment, and peace?

"Reading about nature is fine, but if a person walks in the woods and listens carefully, he can learn more than what is in books, for they speak with the voice of God."

— George Washington Carver (early 1860s – 1943)

6

Dr. Sleeth says, "Every one of those beautiful trees that gave syrup, that put on a spectacular color show in the fall, that shaded us in the summer, was a gift to the future from those who came before us. Those people taught by example. And their lining the road with trees is a sermon about faith."

What are some other "sermons about faith" left to us by previous generations? What "sermons about faith" would you like to leave for future generations?

A CHANGED HEART = A CHANGED LIFE

When I worked at a boarding school, I joined a faculty "green team." With the help of two other teachers, we started a paper-recycling program. Students made recycling boxes and asked teachers if they would keep one in each of their rooms. At the end of the week, one of my colleagues arranged to park a school van in a central location. The students in my morning class went around campus offering to collect boxes that had not yet been emptied, and then I drove the van to the recycling center during my lunch break.

The next fall, we expanded our program to include bottles and cans. We obtained blue trash barrels to put around the campus. The industrial arts program drilled a hole in the center of each top, and a student painted "Cans and Bottles Only" around the hole.

To make the recycling programs a permanent fixture of campus culture, we invited the National Honor Society to take responsibility for bottles and cans. Because there is a five-cent deposit on all beverage containers in the state, the club could collect the redemption money and donate it to a good cause. We then asked the dean of the freshman class if his students would take on paper recycling as an ongoing service project. He agreed, and thereafter responsibility for the recycling program was handed down to each entering freshman class.

Our school also had a senior capstone program. The purpose of the senior capstone was to select an area of personal interest and complete a semester-long research project "capped" by a practical, service-oriented application. One of my first students wrote a proposal to switch the entire campus to 30-percent recycled paper. When the student demonstrated that it would not cost the school any more money to be more environmentally responsible, the headmaster immediately approved the change. He also promised to switch to the slightly more expensive 100-percent postconsumer recycled content paper once it could be demonstrated that paper usage on campus — and paper costs — had decreased.

At another student's suggestion, the school's head librarian, a member of our faculty green team, switched the default print setting on the library printers from single-sided to double-sided. Paper costs in the library dropped from $9,000 to less than $4,500 in one year — more than twice the savings needed to make a campus switch to 100-percent recycled paper cost neutral.

Another advocate on the green team was a young physics teacher. Working with a nonprofit environmental education program, her class conducted a campus-wide energy audit. The class chose three lighting projects to research and made recommendations in a formal proposal to the administration. All three of the recommended changes — switching to LED lights in exit signs, using motion-detector lighting in selected classrooms, and installing dimmers in the cafeteria where natural lighting was abundant — were immediately approved. The students were commended for proposing changes that were cost effective as well as good for the environment — a lesson not only in physics but also in the rewards of civic involvement.

Even several years later initiatives continue to be proposed and approved — including cutting back on Styrofoam use in the cafeteria and composting cafeteria food waste. The entire waste disposal system was reevaluated, and large glass, plastics, and metal recycling collection sites were installed around campus. As a result, trash production on campus has been reduced by 50 percent.

These students learned by asking questions, researching answers, proposing solutions, and doing. Faculty taught by doing, not just saying. And the entire school became an *example*, with trickle down to students' homes. Instead of being satisfied with what has been accomplished, the school community sees learning as an *ongoing journey*. And the lessons they have learned are being passed along as a *legacy* to future generations of students.

Today, "green" is not only the school's official color — it's also an integral part of the campus culture. The school motto, *Semper Discens* (always learning), applies not only to what we know but also to how we live.

—Nancy Sleeth

Adapted with permission from *Go Green, Save Green: A Simple Guide to Saving Time, Money, and God's Green Earth* (Tyndale, 2009).

GOOD STEWARD ACTION PLAN: TEACH
Instructions

1. Pick two or more new actions from the suggested lists to commit to today and this year — or come up with your own way to teach others about creation care.
2. Go to blessedearth.org and join our community of Good Stewards. Explore the website to find additional ideas for saving energy and becoming a better steward of God's creation.
3. We will send you encouragements throughout the year and help you stay on track with your goals. As disciple-makers, we're all in this together, so share your journey. Let us know what was easy, what was difficult, and inspire others with your story!

TODAY, LORD, HELP ME TO:
Pick at least two of the following goals, or come up with your own actions.

○ Teach by example.
○ Pray that everyone involved in our children's education, myself included, learns to model healthier stewardship practices.
○ Make good stewardship choices on behalf of those in my household or under my care.
○ Go on a nature walk and invite someone to join me.

1. _____

2. _____

THIS YEAR, LORD, HELP ME TO:
Pick at least two of the following goals, or come up with your own actions.

- ○ Continue to teach by example.
- ○ Ask friends about carpooling to school and after-school activities; encourage kids to walk/bike to school more often.
- ○ Call my children's schools to find out if they're using natural cleaning products; if they're not, recommend some options and encourage them to make the switch.
- ○ Find out if the printers in the school's computer lab are set to double-sided default; if they're not, encourage the school to make the change and explain the savings involved.
- ○ Encourage kids to take responsibility for caring for God's earth and empower them to share their ideas on how their school can help care for the planet.
- ○ Offer to bring one or more live plants to offices, churches, or school classrooms.
- ○ Donate paper products made from recycled paper to classrooms; educate others about the difference it can make.
- ○ Reuse backpacks instead of buying new ones; encourage kids to donate old or unused backpacks, bags, and clothing to The Salvation Army, Goodwill, or a local homeless ministry.

1. _____

2. _____

"If I ever start feeling too complacent in my creation care journey, all I need to do is open my Bible. If we approach God in humility and listen for His voice, His Word is an endless source of learning, growth, and knowledge. God's Word challenges me to ask questions, seek wisdom, and follow the example of our Savior, Jesus Christ."

—Matthew Sleeth

HOPE

SESSION SUMMARY

> *"[T]hose who hope in the LORD will renew their
> strength. They will soar on wings like eagles;
> they will run and not grow weary, they will walk
> and not be faint."*
>
> **—Isaiah 40:31 NIV**

When Christians talk about "going green" or "saving the planet,"
they bring something unique to the discussion: hope. Not just
hope for a better future someday in heaven, but hope for today
through the power of God's Holy Spirit at work in His church.
We hope and pray for a better world, and then we act as if it will
become a reality. Combine faith, hope, and love, and things get
done. Change happens.

The real proof of the power of the gospel of Jesus Christ is
its power to change lives.

As believers in Christ, we are in the life business—life today,
life tomorrow, and life the next day. Yes, at the resurrection you
will get a new body. Yes, one day there will be a new earth. But
these vessels and this planet are not disposable or worthless.
We aren't supposed to do just anything we want to them; we are
God's assigned caretakers.

As imperfect as we humans are at the practice of faith, hope, and love, we have all experienced their ability to transform us. Our theology and, more importantly, our relationship with Jesus, drives us to care for our Father's planet and all His children.

The body of Christ was redeemed to be the hands and feet of God at work in the world, and where the hands and feet of God are at work, there is hope for creation and for all of humanity.

REFLECTIONS ON HOPE

One of my favorite children's books is The Little Engine That Could. The story is about a big train that breaks down while carrying a load of toys and other good things to children who live on the other side of a mountain. The broken-down engine asks several other passing trains for help, but they are either unable or unwilling. Finally, he sees a tiny blue engine, and asks that (much smaller) engine if he'll pull the shipment of good things to the children on the other side of the mountain. The little train looks up at that huge mountain and the heavy shipment, and isn't sure he's up to the task. But finally he decides to give it a go. And all the way up the hill, our little hero puffs, "I think I can. I think I can. I think I can."

Like that little train, we may feel like there's a huge mountain standing between us and the greener, cleaner world we long for. But Jesus had a few words for us about mountains. In Matthew 17:20, He says, "If you have faith as small as a mustard seed, you can say to this mountain, 'Move from here to there,' and it will move. Nothing will be impossible for you." With faith in God, nothing is impossible.

Living a green life is within the reach of every one of us. I think you can. God thinks you can. When the children from the next "valley"—from the next generation—see us and the world we pass on to them, my hope is that they'll see a generation that was green. My hope is that they'll see a generation that took its choices seriously, that placed its faith in God, and found the strength to climb the highest mountain. My hope is that they'll see a little generation that did.

—Emma Sleeth

Adapted with permission from It's Easy Being Green (Youth Specialties/ Zondervan, 2008).

SESSION NOTES: HOPE

As you watch the final session film, *Hope*, use the space below to jot down notes, thoughts, and questions.

SESSION QUESTIONS: HOPE

1

Hope isn't the first reaction most people have when considering the world's problems. Do the world's environmental problems seem overwhelming to you? How do you typically react when problems seem overwhelming? How does hope change your attitude?

"We see highways that get wider, more crowded, and more numerous. There are fewer and fewer flocks of birds in the sky. And if that doesn't get you down, just listen to predictions about the world's dwindling rainforests or freshwater supplies. All of this can be overwhelming—it can be depressing."

—Dr Matthew Sleeth

2

Dr. Sleeth suggests that, as Christians, "We hope and pray for a better world, and then we act as if it will become a reality." Why are hope and faith so crucial to the environmental movement? What environmental changes do you hope and pray for? Do you act as if they will become a reality? Explain.

3

How could changing our lives to take better care of the environment serve as a witness for the gospel?

"The power of the Bible doesn't lie in its ability to be proven scientifically, logically, or archaeologically. The real proof of the gospel is its power to change lives."

—Dr. Matthew Sleeth

4

Dr. Sleeth suggests "the church brings unique contributions to creation care." What contributions can the church bring to resolving environmental problems?

5

In what sense is caring for the planet intertwined with our call to feed the hungry and care for the poor? If we would call 911 to save a life, why aren't we (metaphorically) calling 911 to save *all* life?

"During our time on earth, we act as the body of Christ, as the hands and feet of life on the planet. If it means calling 911 when someone is having a heart attack, we should help. If it means feeding the hungry or clothing the naked, we do it. If it means cleaning up the water so the fish don't have mercury or dioxin, the body of Christ is called to action."

—Dr. Matthew Sleeth

6 ─────────────────────────────────

What factors have contributed to our "dullness" toward the environment? How can the church help us awaken and "rise vigorously toward justice"? How can "falling in love with creation deeper and deeper" help us "respond to its endangerment with passion"?

"We shall awaken from our dullness and rise vigorously toward justice. If we fall in love with creation deeper and deeper, we will respond to its endangerment with passion."

— Hildegard of Bingen (1098 – 1179)

7 ─────────────────────────────────

How can you help "bring new life into all that has been created"?

"In a time of ecological emergency, the church can offer to the world a hope that is rooted in the power of God to bring new life into all that has been created."
— Wesley Granberg-Michaelson (b. 1945), *Ecology and Life*

A CHANGED HEART = A CHANGED LIFE

Christ the Gardener has returned! This is the good news: God's plan for redemption of the earth is no less bold or powerful than His original creative one. The difference is that although we were not part of His original creative team, we are invited onto the redemptive one.

In the gospel of Luke, a well-educated man asks Christ point-blank, "What must I do to inherit eternal life?" Jesus' answer sums up all of Scripture, and may be the most instructive passage regarding the world's environmental problems: "You shall love the Lord your God with all your heart, and with all your soul, and with all your strength, and with all your mind; and your neighbor as yourself" (Luke 10:27).

The questioner then asks, "Who is my neighbor?" In reply, Christ tells a story. A Jewish man is going down from Jerusalem to Jericho when he falls into the hands of robbers who strip him, beat him, and leave him "half dead." Jesus then says a priest from the man's own religious group walks by the wounded man lying in the road, but offers no assistance. A second religious man comes along, a Levite. He sees the man, but instead of helping, crosses to the other side of the road and continues walking. Finally, a third man comes along, traveling on a donkey. He is a Samaritan, an ethnic and religious group despised by the Jews, and vice versa. But the Samaritan man is moved by compassion. He gets off his donkey and begins making bandages, using his own oil and wine to help the man. He then puts the wounded man on his donkey and pays for care at an inn, the equivalent of a hospital in that day. Lastly he agrees to pick up the bill for any additional care. Then Jesus asks his questioner: "Which of these three do you think was a neighbor to the man who fell into the hands of robbers?"

As an ER physician, I saw some 30,000 patients. Only once did someone come in and pay the hospital bill for a stranger.

This parable demonstrates a continuum of compassion, which can be applied to many problems, including the environment. The priest represents those of us who refuse to take any responsibility for environmental problems, even though we claim a close relationship with God. We close our eyes and walk on by. The second passerby, the Levite, is like most of us: he sees the problem, then says, "I should get back to Jerusalem and raise awareness. Maybe I'll blog on the problem of highway muggings, or send a letter off to the Roman centurion about beefing up patrols and installing better street lights." Like the Levite, we see the hardship caused by environmental problems, particularly for the poorest among us. Our hearts are moved to compassion, but we do little, if anything, to help because we don't want to be inconvenienced. Only the Samaritan, the one who is least likely to view the fallen Jewish man as his neighbor, takes action. He saw the need, and had mercy on him. Jesus tells us, as he told his questioner, "Go and do likewise."

What does this parable teach us about how we should approach environmental problems today? To have any lasting effect, our hearts must be moved by compassion for our fellow man and all of God's creation. We may find it dangerous. We may have to use our own resources. It may be inconvenient. It may be expensive. We may be ridiculed. We will have to take ongoing responsibility and make personal sacrifices. But such is the path to eternal life.

Everyone is our neighbor, including foreigners, strangers, people who hate us, and future generations. Perhaps the most important lesson of the Good Samaritan — the action that can separate us from the priest and Levite — is that we must "get off our donkey" before we can become part of the solution. The future will not be saved by our good intentions. It will be made better, or worse, only by our actions.

We show our love for the Lord by loving our neighbors. Every time we buy anything, or take any action, our family now asks two questions: Will this help me love God? And will this help me love my neighbor? The answer will always lead us to right action.

If we take shorter showers, carpool, or plant a tree, no one will necessarily notice or thank us. But if these things are done as an act to serve the Lord and to protect our neighbors, then we will have grown as loving, spiritual beings. Love is the great hope that the church offers the environmental movement.

— Dr. Matthew Sleeth

Adapted with permission from *The Green Bible* (HarperOne, 2008).

GOOD STEWARD ACTION PLAN: HOPE

Instructions

In this final session, we will work on a comprehensive plan for action. Look over your previous goals, and select actions that will help you meet major goals in the months ahead.

For more ideas, visit the Resources page at blessedearth.org. In addition, *Go Green, Save Green* (www.gogreenthebook.com) has thousands of practical ideas that you can incorporate into your plan.

As the hands and feet of God, we have a responsibility to love what God loves and do what God does. My prayer is that, individually and together, we're faithful. In God's power and by His leading, hope starts here.

TODAY, LORD, HELP ME TO:

Select and accomplish two major goals (choose some of the examples below or write your own).

O Reduce my energy use by at least 10 percent.
O Cut back on trash production at home by 50 percent.
O Lead a Sunday school class using these films and the guide-book discussion questions.
O Start a green team at work, school, or church.
O Plan a community event or host a screening of the Blessed Earth films to raise awareness and inspire change.
O Organize an Earth Day Sunday event at church.
O Start a creation care column in my church bulletin.

1. _____

2. _____

Lord, help me *achieve these goals* through specific actions:

GOAL 1:

Specific actions that will help me achieve this goal:

1. _____

2. _____

3. _____

4. _____

5. _____

GOAL 2:

Specific actions that will help me achieve this goal:

1. _____

2. _____

3. _____

4. _____

5. _____

"The Bible makes it clear that our hope isn't just hope in heaven or faith that better days are coming someday in eternity, but faith in the real presence and power of the Holy Spirit at work in and through us today to do what, without Him, would be impossible. It is only through God's power that we have the strength or ability to do God's will, whether it's making disciples or working to protect and share the resources He's given us. In God's power, we have hope that it is possible to tend and protect the garden He's placed us in."

—Dr. Matthew Sleeth

ACKNOWLEDGMENTS

This book couldn't have happened without the creative genius of Santino Stoner and David Wenzel. God led us to break bread with you nearly three years ago along the river near Grand Rapids; thank you for your strength and perseverance as we paddled upstream together.

Brett and Corey — we are grateful for your immense talents and your friendship. To the entire Dot&Cross dream team — including Sue, Seth, Michael, and Sally — your belief in our work keeps us going.

We also thank God for our partners at Zondervan — especially John Raymond, Michael Cook, and Sandra Vander Zicht — we are grateful for your willingness to walk with us in faith.

To our partners at HarperOne — including Mickey Maudlin, Emily Grandstaff, and Marlene Baer — thanks for believing in the creation care message and helping us share it with the world.

To our friends and neighbors at Asbury Seminary — including Tom Tumblin, Ginny Proctor, Leslie Andrews, Ellsworth Kallas, and Tim Tennent — it is an honor to reach out to God's kingdom alongside of you.

To Will Sears: you are an answer to prayer. Blessed Earth is indeed blessed by your many talents.

Finally, our loving thanks to the Kendeda Foundation: your generosity, encouragement, and faithful support of Blessed Earth have helped us move mountains.

ABOUT
BLESSED EARTH

Blessed Earth is an educational nonprofit that inspires and equips faith communities to become better stewards of the earth. Through outreach to churches, campuses, and media we build bridges that promote measurable environmental change and meaningful spiritual growth.

The Sleeth family's environmental journey has paralleled their faith journey. As they began to live out what it means to love God with all their heart, mind, soul, and strength, and to love their neighbors as themselves, they found their calling: to live more simply. The first and most important miracle for the Sleeths is that their entire family came to know Christ, not just in their heads but in their daily actions. Hanging clothes on the line, washing dishes by hand, and growing their own food are all ways of how they show daily respect for God's creation, and love for their global neighbors.

From these humble beginnings a revolutionary ministry began to grow. Dr. Sleeth wrote a book that received a much wider, more enthusiastic response than he could have ever dreamed. Then, to address larger audiences and respond to the hundreds of speaking requests, the Sleeths formed Blessed Earth. The Sleeths' message has inspired congregations, colleges, and individuals that never had creation care on their radar screen to make huge changes, quickly. When people embrace the principles of simplicity and conservation in their hearts, the difference is dramatic.

Focusing less on material things, and more on relationships with family, friends, and God, leads to happier, more meaningful, and richer lives. With God, all things are possible — including a cleaner, healthier world to leave for future generations.

ADDITIONAL RESOURCES

Also available from the Sleeths and Blessed Earth:

Serving God, Saving the Planet
(Zondervan, 2007)

Dr. Matthew Sleeth and his family lived in a big house on the coast, had two luxury cars, and many material possessions. As chief of the medical staff at a large hospital, Sleeth was living the American dream — until he saw an increasing number of his patients suffering from cancer, asthma, and other chronic diseases. Suspecting that the earth and its inhabitants were in trouble, he turned to Jesus for guidance. Dr. Sleeth shares how his family cut their use of resources by more than two-thirds and discovered how the scriptural lessons of personal responsibility, simplicity, and stewardship could lead to a healthier, more joyful life.

Go Green, Save Green
(Tyndale, 2009)

Many people want to "go green" but put it off because they believe it's too time consuming and too expensive. Not so! Nancy Sleeth and her family have been living an eco-friendly lifestyle for years, saving both time and money. Now, for the first time, she divulges hundreds of practical, easy-to-implement steps that you can take to create substantial money savings while protecting the earth.

It's Easy Being Green
(Zondervan/Youth Specialties, 2008)

Want to set your teens on fire for Christ and all of creation? Just fifteen years old when she wrote *It's Easy Being Green*, author/activist Emma Sleeth is a rebel with a cause: saving souls while saving the planet. With real stories from real life, Emma explores how everything we do—from what we eat to how we spend our spare time—impacts the world.

The Gospel According to the Earth
(HarperOne, 2010)

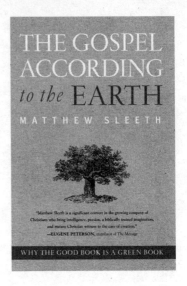

In *The Gospel According to the Earth*, Matthew Sleeth retells the often radically countercultural Bible stories that motivated his journey from emergency room doctor to environmental leader, and shows Christians what they can do to care for God's green earth. With passion and faith, Sleeth provides a new green lens through which we can read the Bible to discover answers to the biggest questions of our time and helps us to see afresh how relevant, broad, and deep the Bible's teaching remains.

For more information about the Creation Care journey, visit blessedearth. org, where you'll find the most comprehensive, interactive Creation Care resources on the web.